# ALBERT SCHWEITZER'S REVERENCE FOR LIFE

*For Shannon, Sonia and Nicole,*
*and in memory of Kurt and Alice Bergel*

# Albert Schweitzer's Reverence for Life

## Ethical Idealism and Self-Realization

MIKE W. MARTIN
*Chapman University, USA*

ASHGATE

Published by
Ashgate Publishing Limited
Gower House
Croft Road
Aldershot
Hampshire GU11 3HR
England

Ashgate Publishing Company
Suite 420
101 Cherry Street
Burlington, VT 05401-4405
USA

Ashgate website: http://www.ashgate.com

**British Library Cataloguing in Publication Data**
Martin, Mike W., 1946-
Albert Schweitzer's reverence for life : ethical idealism and self-realization
1. Schweitzer, Albert, 1875-1965 - Ethics 2. Schweitzer, Albert, 1875-1965 - Knowledge - Environmentalism
I. Title
179.1'092

**Library of Congress Cataloging-in-Publication Data**
Martin, Mike W., 1946-
Albert Schweitzer's reverence for life : ethical idealism and self-realization / Mike W. Martin.
p. cm.
Includes bibliographical references and index.
ISBN 978-0-7546-6106-1 (hardcover : alk. paper) 1. Schweitzer, Albert, 1875-1965. 2. Ethics, Modern--20th century. I. Title.

B2430.S374M37 2007
170.92--dc22

2006101694

ISBN-13: 978-0-7546-6106-1

Printed and bound in Great Britain by Antony Rowe Ltd, Chippenham, Wiltshire.

# Contents

# Preface

I read Albert Schweitzer's *Out of My Life and Thought* and *The Primeval Forest* as a high-school student planning to become a physician. In college my interests changed to philosophy, but I studied Schweitzer's ethics only after I began teaching at Chapman University. There Schweitzer was literally imprinted on the campus, with quotations from his writings engraved on ground plaques in front of benches, memorabilia from his Lambaréné hospital displayed in the library and student union, and annual awards given in his name to prominent philanthropists. This presence was due primarily to Kurt Bergel, a professor of history who taught a course on Schweitzer with his wife Alice, a professor of German. My involvement in that course was the initial catalyst for this book.

Schweitzer's life of service as a physician in Africa, for which he received the Nobel Peace Prize, is deservedly celebrated and emulated, albeit contested by post-colonial theorists, but his innovative moral philosophy remains neglected. Even philosophers who appreciate his pioneering contributions to environmental ethics rarely understand them in the wider context of the ethical theory he called reverence for life. In this book I offer a new interpretation and assessment of reverence for life as an ethical idealism of self-realization, love and nature-centred spirituality.

I benefited from conversations with students and colleagues, especially Kurt Bergel, Alice Bergel, Paul Delp, Ron Huntington, Marv Meyer, Anita Storck and Virginia Warren. I also learned from visiting speakers who include Ara Paul Barsam, James Brabazon, Norman Cousins, Erich Graesser, Louise Jilek-Aall, Antje Bultmann Lemke, Nikki Lindberg, Sylvere Mbondobari, Linus Pauling and James M. Robinson. Many of these thinkers spoke at a 1999 conference organized by Kurt Bergel and Marv Meyer, 'Schweitzer at the Turn of the Millennium'. Rhena Schweitzer Miller, the daughter of Albert and Hélène Bresslau Schweitzer, was an inspiring presence at the conference and returned on other occasions to Chapman.

Amy Rudometkin provided highly professional assistance, and librarians Gina Wilkinson and Claudia Horn provided valuable research assistance. A one-semester sabbatical from Chapman University helped me complete the manuscript.

Above all, I thank my wife Shannon for daily conversations that clarified my thoughts, and for the love that sustains me.

# Acknowledgements

Chapter 7 (with a small part of Chapter 8) was published in a different version as 'Good Fortune Obligates: Gratitude, Philanthropy, and Colonialism', *Southern Journal of Philosophy*, 37 (1999): 57–75. It is used by permission of the editor. Chapter 4 was published in an earlier version as 'Rethinking Reverence for Life', *Between the Species*, 9 (1993): 204–13.

I am grateful to Rhena Schweitzer Miller for permission to quote from: Albert Schweitzer, *The Philosophy of Civilization*, trans. C.T. Campion (Amherst, NY: Prometheus Books, 1987); and Albert Schweitzer, *Out of My Life and Thought: An Autobiography*, trans. A.B. Lemke (New York: Henry Holt and Company, 1990), and reprinted by Johns Hopkins University Press, 1998.

# Chapter 1

# Introduction

> The maintenance of one's own life at the highest level by becoming more and more perfect in spirit, and the maintenance at the highest level of other life by sympathetic, helpful self-devotion to it – this is ethics.[1]

Albert Schweitzer, who lived from 1875 to 1965, sets forth an innovative moral perspective centred on self-realization, nature-centred spirituality and ethical idealism. Responding to a culture of violence and alienation, he regards ethics as a deeply personal response to needs for meaning and self-fulfilment. Pioneering an environmental ethics, he affirms the sacredness of life in its diversity and unity, linking ethics to spirituality without religious dogma. And anticipating the contemporary renaissance of virtue ethics, he makes ideals of character fundamental while celebrating individualism and wide tolerance in applying those ideals. Reverence for life emerges from the will to live present in each of us, widens by affirming our kinship with other life, and unfolds in a moral optimism of self-realization through service to others and the pursuit of excellence.

Reverence for life, as Schweitzer calls his moral perspective, is now widely appreciated in environmental ethics. Even there, however, it is not understood within the full context of his ethics of self-realization and ethical idealism. Moreover, Schweitzer's ethics is incomplete. The demands of working as a jungle doctor and hospital administrator permitted completion of only two of the four planned volumes of *The Philosophy of Civilization*, his primary philosophical work, although he fleshed out his ideas in many additional writings. My aim is to offer a fresh interpretation that reveals the importance of his moral philosophy while shedding new light on his environmental ethics. In places I also raise criticisms and suggest revisions, agreeing with Schweitzer that we honour a system of thought by testing it rigorously for its truth.[2]

The phrase 'reverence for life' came to Schweitzer in 1915 while on a medical journey upstream from his hospital at Lambaréné in French Equatorial Africa.[3] Reverence combines respect and awe, ethics and spirituality. Life includes humans, animals and plants, taken as individuals and as interconnected. The meaning of the phrase is not self-evident, however, and Schweitzer was dismayed when it became a catchphrase rather than an invitation to explore his writings. 'The phrase is related to a whole line of thought', he insists, and it must be understood in terms of 'the purpose and the meaning of my work as a whole'.[4] That body of work is more complex than appears at first glance.

To be sure, Schweitzer strives for simplicity, convinced that 'whatever is deep is also simple'.[5] He frequently encapsulates his ethics of reverence for life in epigrams; for example, 'it is good to maintain and to encourage life; it is bad to destroy life or to obstruct it.'[6] Nevertheless, the epigrams are intended to illuminate the ideals that should guide our responses to moral dilemmas, not to deny that perplexing dilemmas arise when the myriad moral reasons come into conflict. Indeed, reverence for life adds complexity by elevating moral demands and widening the circle of moral concern to include all life.[7] Even the phrase 'reverence for life' has multiple meanings: it names a unifying moral aspiration (a multifaceted ideal), an umbrella character trait (a multifaceted virtue), a foundational principle of responsibility (a multifaceted obligation), and Schweitzer's moral perspective in its entirety (an ethical theory).[8]

As an ethical theory, reverence for life has three focal points: self-realization, nature-centred spirituality and ethical idealism. First, self-realization combines striving for excellence with sharing in others' lives. Excellence, like ethics itself, demands a deep sincerity with ourselves (authenticity) concerning what we care about most deeply. Ultimately, that caring is rooted in and unfolds our will to live – that is, our desires to survive, to affirm ourselves, and to pursue self-realization inspired by ideals. Because we are social creatures whose lives are intimately interwoven with others, sincerity involves forming personal projects of love – projects that express caring in a highly personal manner. The projects of love include those of family, profession, philanthropy, voluntary service and the pursuit of excellence in all other desirable endeavours.

Second, reverence for life grounds ethics in a nature-centred spirituality. As discussed in Chapter 2, Schweitzer abandons conventional religious dogma and is largely agnostic about a supernatural deity. Yet he is a profoundly spiritual thinker who affirms all life as sacred, at least in its creative aspects. He articulates an *ethical mysticism* whereby we achieve spiritual unity with other lives through active caring in the spirit of the unity of life and the preciousness of each life. Acts of sympathetic support have symbolic and spiritual meaning in bringing unity and peace into a world of conflict and violence. By widening the circle of moral concern to include all life, reverence for life completes the ethics of love embedded in world religions: 'Reverence for Life is the ethic of love widened into universality.'[9] At the same time, reverence for life is firmly rooted in this world. It emerges from the will to live found in each of us – our will to survive, develop and connect sympathetically with other life.[10] Chapter 4 explores the implications of ethical mysticism, or what might be called *biotheism*, for environmental ethics.

Third, reverence for life is an ethics of ideals of goodness, including both moral goodness and non-moral goodness such as aesthetic appreciation and scientific understanding. It is a version of what philosophers call ethical idealism or (more misleadingly) perfectionism. As a unifying ideal, reverence for life does not replace the myriad specific ideals defining self-realization and responsibilities to others. Instead, it yokes them together and widens their scope. Likewise, as an umbrella virtue, reverence for life draws together and unifies more specific virtues, including 'every kind of valuable enthusiasm'.[11]

In his published writings, Schweitzer devotes special attention to five moral ideals and their corresponding virtues: authenticity, compassion, gratitude, justice and peace loving. Authenticity (or sincerity with oneself) demands the full and balanced development of our talents on the basis of honesty with ourselves and within a framework of moral ideals. Compassion is manifested in the human 'fellowship of those who bear the mark of pain' and also in the 'community of suffering' connecting all creatures. Gratitude underlies the principle that 'good fortune obligates', an ideal of reciprocal giving and service that has broad significance. Justice is understood in terms of human rights, which illustrates that Schweitzer appreciates the special moral status of humanity even as he widens the circle of moral concern to include all living organisms. And peace loving implies a commitment to resolve conflicts without violence – although Schweitzer is not the unconditional pacifist he is usually taken to be. His emphasis on these particular virtues is important, and a chapter is devoted to each of them. It should be borne in mind, however, that his ethics of self-realization and ethical idealism is intended to embrace all valid moral virtues, indeed all ideals of excellence that define what he called civilization.

Reverence for life is not an amorphous affirmation of living creatures that leaves us without practical guidance. It is true, and important to note, that Schweitzer renounces the traditional philosophical obsession with moral rules that tell us exactly what to do and with ethical dilemmas that arise when rules come into conflict. Nevertheless, as Chapter 3 discusses, reverence for life provides moral guidance through specific ideals that function as signposts in a morally complex and ambiguous world. In addition, these specific ideals enter into personal projects of love that structure our lives. These projects require the 'widest possible freedom' to interpret and implement moral ideals in pursuing self-fulfilment.[12] Schweitzer's ethics is thus highly individualistic, but only within a framework of justified moral ideals and virtues.

At the same time, Schweitzer is more concerned with moral motivation than with prescribing detailed guidance. To this end, he seeks an *elemental ethics* that is simple, close to experience, rooted in natural desires, strongly motivating, and responsive to needs for meaning.[13] An ethics of self-realization and ideals is flexible yet demanding in order to serve as a popular philosophy contributing to civilization.[14] It also needs to be presented effectively. Schweitzer's presentation combines theory with practice, inspiration with argument, and mystic evocations with reasoning. These combinations add power to his writing, although sometimes they generate problems of interpretation.

Additional interpretive challenges concern how to distinguish between (a) the requirements of reverence for life, as an ethical theory and an umbrella ideal allowing wide moral autonomy in interpreting and applying more specific ideals, and (b) Schweitzer's personal interpretations and applications of specific moral ideals. Usually he simply states his views, at times leaving us unclear whether he intends general requirements or instead his personal applications – applications with which we might reasonably disagree in exercising our moral autonomy. For example, when he rescues caterpillars and mosquitoes, and when he objects to cutting flowers to put in vases, is he implying that reverence for life mandates similar responses from all of us? In linking ethics and spirituality, does he intend that we share his agnosticism about a supernatural deity, or could theists and atheists alike embrace his moral perspective? And is his (highly qualified) defence of early twentieth-century colonialism somehow implied by reverence for life? Even if he does intend these things, can we show that the central tenets of his ethical theory actually leave wider latitude for differences among reasonable persons?

Here, responses to these questions will be provided as we proceed, usually by highlighting the individualistic spirit of reverence for life that leaves room for each of us to apply ideals in a responsible but personal manner. Note, however, that such interpretative challenges are not unusual. Most philosophers do not neatly separate the mandatory elements in their ethical theories from their personal applications of the theory, and most of them have moral blind spots. Aristotle's misogynist discussion of character and acceptance of slavery, Thomas Jefferson's racism in applying human rights, and Immanuel Kant's parochial views of sex are only a few of many examples. Even when thinkers see their own moral situation clearly, their ethical theories need to be adjusted to different historical settings. In any case, we should not confuse reverence for life with reverence for Schweitzer, as he would be the first to insist.

One thing is clear. For Schweitzer, philosophy matters. Notice the title he gives to the opening chapter of *The Philosophy of Civilization*: 'How Philosophy is Responsible for the Collapse of Civilization'. We laugh, for the title might have been written by Woody Allen or Monty Python – as if philosophy could have any such cultural importance! Schweitzer believes it does. For him, the primary task of philosophy is to articulate values that give meaning to our lives and advance civilization.[15] He seeks to 'throw the belief in a new humanity, like a torch, into our dark age'.[16]

## Notes

1 Albert Schweitzer, *Indian Thought and Its Development*, trans. Mrs Charles E.B. Russell (Gloucester, MA: Peter Smith, 1977), p. 260.
2 Ibid., p. viii.
3 Albert Schweitzer, *Out of My Life and Thought*, trans. Antje Bultmann Lemke (Baltimore,MD: Johns Hopkins University Press, 1998), p. 155.
4 Norman Cousins, *Albert Schweitzer's Mission* (New York: W.W. Norton, 1985), p. 75.
5 Albert Schweitzer, *Philosophy of Civilization*, trans. C.T. Campion (Amherst, NY: Prometheus Books, 1987), p. 7.
6 Ibid., p. 309.
7 Schweitzer, *Indian Thought and Its Development*, p. 261.
8 Carl Wellman distinguishes some of these meanings in 'An Analysis of Reverence for Life', *Journal of Value Inquiry*, 11 (1977): 46–8.
9 Schweitzer, *Out of My Life and Thought*, p. 235.
10 Albert Schweitzer, 'The Ethics of Reverence for Life', *Christendom*, 1 (1936): 227.
11 Schweitzer, Philosophy of Civilization, p. 311.
12 Ibid., pp. 334–5.
13 Schweitzer, *Out of My Life and Thought*, p. 228.
14 Schweitzer, *Philosophy of Civilization*, pp. 3, 283.
15 Ibid., p. xiv.
16 Ibid., p. 84.

# Chapter 2

# Ethics from Within

An instinctive reverence for life is within us, for we are will-to-live.[1]

As an ethical theory, reverence for life responds to our needs for meaning and moral motivation. It grounds ethics in instincts for survival, self-affirmation, self-realization and sympathy, as well as in cumulative moral experience and philosophical reflection. Together, our reason and empathy lead us to appreciate our kinship with other living organisms, gradually developing into an *ethical mysticism* in which we experience unity with all life whenever we contribute to even one life in a spirit of reverence. In this way, reverence for life is a 'natural ethic' that expresses our 'physiological make-up' and yet 'arrives at the noblest spirituality'.[2]

## Will-to-Live Argument

The will-to-live argument attempts to justify widening the moral circle to include all living organisms. In doing so, it presents ethics as 'the very manifestation of our will-to-live'.[3] Although Schweitzer presents the argument in several slightly different versions, here is its basic structure.[4]

1. *Self-awareness*: I am aware that I will to live – to survive, seek pleasure, avoid harm, develop and affirm myself.

   Our most intimate self-consciousness is not Descartes' abstraction 'I think, therefore I am.' Instead, it is that we will to live. Even to say 'I am life' is somewhat too abstract as a starting point, for 'life' is a mystery we do not understand.[5] Instead, we experience ourselves as alive – as a cluster of strivings to continue living, experience pleasure and joy, avoid pain and diminishment, develop our interests and abilities, and affirm ourselves. These strivings are instinctive but not blind, for our will to live includes our reason – our ability to perceive and understand, to value and evaluate.
2. *Instinctive sympathy*: I have instinctive tendencies to feel empathy, sympathy, compassion and caring toward at least some other lives, both human and non-human.

   Our self-awareness includes awareness of other lives: 'I am life which wills to live, in the midst of life which wills to live.'[6] In varying ways and degrees, we take an interest in other lives, responding with empathy, sympathy and compassion. Empathy is sensitivity in light of our similarities and shared identity with other vibrant and vulnerable creatures. Sympathy and compassion are caring responses to the suffering and misfortunes of other life. Caring includes all these responses together with the simple delight in sharing in the lives of others.

3. *Resignation*: In humility, I accept my dependency while cherishing the freedom to shape my values and life plan.

   Resignation means accepting our contingency and vulnerability. At the same time, it implies appreciating the spiritual freedom to shape our attitudes, values and activities.[7] As such, resignation is a creative humility, a 'passive self-perfecting' that prepares us for more active self-development. It constitutes the vestibule through which we enter ethics.[8] Resignation also includes humility about human aspirations. From a cosmic perspective we are specks of dust, vulnerable from every direction, destined to die, and able to help others in only limited ways. Rather than prompting despair, however, this humility paves the way for moral commitment.

4. *Reverence for self*: Sincerity with myself deepens my self-affirmation through striving for self-realization.

   Reverence for self is the foundation of reverence for all life. It consists in a deepened self-respect and self-affirmation that emerges from sincerity with ourselves (authenticity), and which combines self-honesty, self-fidelity and integrity.[9] Even staying alive becomes a conscious choice in response to moments of suicidal despair. Beyond survival, we affirm and purposefully pursue self-realization. Our will to live unfolds as striving for self-perfecting in the sense of becoming a 'will to the realizing of ideals'.[10]

5. *Widened sympathy*: Reason and empathy widen my sympathy by recognizing all living organisms as, like me, having (or being) a will to live.

   Our instinctive sympathy is intermittent and weak, compared to instincts for self-preservation and self-development, but they can be 'absorbed by conscious reflection and further developed'.[11] That reflection reveals we are part of life, born of other lives, and dependent on other lives for our existence. Our desires for self-realization and self-perfecting elicit an increased interest in other life.[12]

6. *Reverence for all life*: I experience, develop and manifest the attitude that 'it is good to maintain and to encourage life; it is bad to destroy life or to obstruct it.'[13]

   Moral consistency, which is a product of reason and empathy, requires that my attitude toward other life 'be of a piece with my attitude towards my own life'.[14] Just as I value my life as sacred, I come to value other lives as sacred. Gradually, and in varying degrees, I experience a 'compulsion [that is, a strong desire and felt responsibility] to show to all will-to-live the same reverence as I do to my own'.[15] And just as valuing my life means finding it good to preserve and develop my life, reverence for all life means valuing acts of sharing, saving, helping and enabling other life to achieve its highest development.

This will-to-live argument is not intended as a knock-down proof.[16] Indeed, the steps are overlapping modes of experience, rather than a sequential presentation of evidence. The argument employs an experience-based, phenomenological progression of reasoning based on awareness of needs and values. It presents reverence for life as a reasonable extension of instinctive self-affirmation and empathy for other life. In this way, it reveals how reverence for life develops naturally from within, as a manifestation of our will to live combined with the exercise of reason.

In his search for a natural ethic, Schweitzer does not naively leap from facts to values.[17] He does not infer, for example, that my life is valuable because I desire to live, or that other life is valuable because I feel sympathy for it. Instead, the argument invokes values at every step: development, which alludes to both normal growth and higher aspiration (Step 1); sympathy, caring and compassion (Steps 2 and 5); humility and spiritual acceptance (Step 3); reverence for self, sincerity, honesty with oneself, and fidelity to oneself (Step 4); and good actions involved in reverence for all life (Step 6).

Given the argument's emphasis on natural desires, we might wonder why it was not discovered long ago. The answer is that although the argument is rooted in the instincts it is elaborated in light of reason – 'an understanding that penetrates to the depths of things and that embraces the wholeness of reality, extending even into the realm of the will'.[18] Our reason is in part the product of a long history of moral reflection: 'There are many great souls who have blazed sections of the trail for us.'[19] Schweitzer outlines that history throughout the second volume of *The Philosophy of Civilization*. To mention just a few key thinkers, the emphasis on instinctive sympathy is found in David Hume, Adam Smith and Charles Darwin. Resignation is central to the Stoics, whom Schweitzer greatly admired for the content and style of their philosophy, as in Epictetus' simple expression of creative resignation: 'Some things are up to us and some are not up to us.'[20] Arthur Schopenhauer introduced the expression 'will to live' in his metaphysics and found parallels between life and the universe in its totality. Immanuel Kant, on whom Schweitzer wrote his Ph.D. dissertation, regarded duties of self-respect as paramount and presupposed by all other duties. Goethe, the thinker who most engaged Schweitzer, as well as the lesser-known Alfred Fouillee and Jean Marie Guyau, connect self-realization to an enlightened cherishing of nature. And Jesus, the heroic individual who riveted Schweitzer's moral imagination, set forth the purist vision of spiritual love. All these individuals contributed to our moral understanding in ways encapsulated in the will-to-live argument.

The argument is provocative and suggestive. Self-affirmation is indeed an elemental and widely appealing starting point for thinking about ethics, as agreed by Kant, Jesus (love others *as* you love yourself) and contemporary mental-health professionals. So is natural empathy and sympathy. By calling for attitudes toward other lives to be 'of a piece with' attitudes toward ourselves, and by highlighting empathy for other creatures, the argument provides an illuminating touchstone for an environmental ethics. Chapter 4 discusses whether we should 'widen the circle' of moral concern to include all life, as claimed in Steps 5 and 6. Here we discuss how reverence for life relates to conventional religious beliefs and to the ethics of love embedded in Christianity and other world religions.

## A Spiritual Ethics

Reverence for life is a spiritual ethics, given its emphasis on inwardness, value-centredness, personal meaning and loving relations with other persons and the world.[21] Schweitzer calls it 'ethical mysticism and mystical ethics'.[22] These terms are misleading if they suggest irrationality, for Schweitzer's ethics celebrates human reason. The terms are intended to highlight the spiritual unity with all life that we experience whenever we actively contribute to other lives in a spirit of reverence. In doing so we are not sacrificing ourselves but rather expressing our individuality and pursuing self-realization.

In contrast, traditional 'identity mysticism' is obsessed with relatively brief and passively-experienced moments of merging with a supernatural deity or with infinite Being.[23] Schweitzer is no stranger to such experiences: 'Here in one existence, life as such comes to consciousness of itself. Isolated individual existence ceases. Outside existence floods into ours.'[24] Nevertheless, isolated experiences of merger have moral significance only when they motivate or accompany acts of sharing or helping, and it is these acts that elicit the most important experiences of spiritual unity. Schweitzer's spirituality is profoundly practical.

Is Schweitzer's spirituality based on belief in a supernatural deity? No. Spiritual resignation, as he understands it, requires accepting the limitations of knowledge, and reason enjoins wariness about flights of faith. We cannot know the ultimate purpose of the universe, if any, or the destiny of humanity.[25] We must resign ourselves to uncertainty about the existence of a supernatural deity who structures the universe with cosmic purposes, other supernatural beings (angels, souls), supernatural states (heaven, hell) and the historical and cosmic significance of our lives.[26] Most perplexing, we must live with the painful enigma of how the totality of creative and destructive forces in the universe relates to reverence for life – to the moral–spiritual commitment to promote and preserve life that emerges within us. In this way, Schweitzer's world-view is based not on blind faith but instead on a reasoned and deepened understanding of life. As he puts it, 'world-view is a product of life-view, not vice versa.'[27] This resignation – this 'knowing ignorance' or 'enlightened ignorance' about the ultimate nature of the universe – liberates by putting us in contact with moral and spiritual reality.[28]

I can have no knowledge of a 'divine personality', other than what I 'experience as mysterious Will within myself' as a moral will.[29] To be sure, in his popular writings Schweitzer writes as if God exists, so that we mystically become one with God through acts of caring for others. Yet he confides to fellow scholar Oskar Kraus that he abandoned orthodoxy by age fifteen, after which he continued to use conventional talk about God in order to convey spiritual ideas to a wide audience.[30] He does so, as well, to minimize the anguish he knew his views would cause to people he cares about.[31] In a letter to his future wife, written when he was thirty, he cautions, 'You and I, we must always keep our religion to ourselves, keep it a secret because what God and immortality are for us, others will see only as atheism and negation of the soul.'[32]

Nevertheless, God is not a mere metaphor for Schweitzer, and even in his philosophical writings he speaks of a sacred force or being with which we can unite: 'Our self-devotion to life with a view to furthering it and maintaining it at its highest value constitutes active union with the eternal Being.'[33] Using his preferred philosophical language, borrowed from Schopenhauer, he speaks of a universal (and capitalized) Will to Live (or Creative Will): 'Reverence for life means to be in the grasp of the infinite, inexplicable, forward-urging Will in which all Being is grounded.'[34] This Will to Live, however, is not separate from the world we experience: 'The only reality is the Being which manifests itself in phenomena.'[35] Taken by itself, this statement is sufficiently vague to allow a difference between God and creation, Being and the phenomenal world. More likely, however, the statement expresses a form of pantheism in which the sacred is equated with the universe in its creative aspects.

Schweitzer says he leaves 'pantheism and theism as an unsolved conflict in my soul.'[36] That is, he remains open to the possibility that there might be a supernatural creator, distinct from the creation, though he was agnostic about that possibility. As for pantheism, it is clear that Schweitzer is not a pantheist in the sense of equating the universe with God, for he finds much that is ungodly in the universe – in particular, horrifying suffering and monstrous evil. Moreover, his ascriptions of sacredness are almost always directed towards living organisms, not rocks and rivers. (There are a few puzzling passages in which he writes as if crystals are alive, usually in portraying the drive to perfection inherent in life as reflected more widely in the order of the universe.[37]) Even so, he writes as if he is a pantheist in the different sense of believing that some sort of metaphysical Will to Live is immanent in the creative (valuable) aspects of the natural world, especially in living organisms.[38] Our only direct experience of a personal divinity, however, is the will to love which we experience within.[39]

All this leads me to agree with Jackson Lee Ice that we 'search in vain for a precise, clear-cut concept of God in Schweitzer'.[40] Nevertheless, one theme stands out. Schweitzer consistently speaks of the sacredness of life – of life in its full diversity and unity but primarily in its creative aspects – a view we might call *biotheism*. Biotheism makes sense of why Schweitzer speaks of life in its unity as a metaphysical force. It makes sense of his repeated statements that we experience the Will to Live inside us, as an instinctive reverence for life – a reverence for both our lives and the lives of others. It is also congruent with his claim that insofar as we promote life we experience 'spiritual union and harmony with the Creative Will which is in and through all'.[41] We experience this Creative Will as the sacred aspects of the universe.

To emphasize, any metaphysical Will to Live cannot be equated with nature or with all aspects of living organisms in their totality, for nature reveals itself as a force that is simultaneously creative (furthering development) and destructive (inimical to life). The relationship between the creative–destructive force in nature and the creative force of love within us remains a permanent enigma.[42] Life is sacred only by virtue of its valuable tendencies to survive, develop and support other life, not in its destructive tendencies to kill and harm. The problem, of course, is that life's creative tendencies require destructive tendencies: life kills other life in order to eat, develop, to feed young, defend territory, and so on. In the final analysis, Schweitzer concludes (and emphasizes) that we cannot fully understand nature spiritually:

Nature 'is wonderfully creative force, and at the same time senselessly destructive force. We face her absolutely perplexed'.[43]

Does reverence for life, as an ethical theory, require us to share Schweitzer's metaphysics, in particular his biotheism and agnosticism about the supernatural? No. Recall the distinction between (a) reverence for life, as an ethical theory that provides wide latitude for personal moral judgment in interpreting and applying moral ideals, and (b) Schweitzer's personal interpretations of moral ideals. Schweitzer's religious views remain of great interest in linking ethics and spirituality. Even so, his primary themes about nature-centred spirituality need not be tied to his religious views. Indeed, his agnosticism about the supernatural is more an expression of personal faith than based on a compelling argument. Reverence for life is an ethics of life-centred spirituality that is compatible with many versions of agnosticism, theism, pantheism and atheism.

For three reasons, then, we can bracket or set aside Schweitzer's agnosticism and metaphysics in understanding the central tenets of reverence for life. First, reverence for life places great emphasis on personal freedom and authenticity in working out our personal worldview and in applying moral ideals, and it enjoins wide tolerance of the varied directions in which authenticity leads. Second, and with equal emphasis, 'Reverence for Life leads us into a spiritual relationship with the world independent of a full understanding of the universe.'[44] Third, Schweitzer's personal religious and metaphysical stance is anything but pellucid, as we have just seen.

What about organized religion? Is Schweitzer recommending that we turn away from participation in churches, synagogues and mosques, perhaps replacing them with nature worship? He is not. Here his views are clear and nuanced. On the one hand, he is critical of the hypocrisies of religious institutions in moral matters, sceptical of religions' pretensions to knowledge about the universe, and dismayed at the power of organized religion to repress the free thought of individuals. On the other hand, he treasures the contribution of responsible religions to moral community.[45] Indeed, sound religion is just ethics, together with spiritual communities that embody and advance ethics.[46] He affirms religions insofar as they are ecumenical and tolerant communities of shared reverence, and he seeks to promote dialogue between Western with Asian religions.

At the same time, Schweitzer regards Jesus as the premier spiritual exemplar and morally heroic human being. Using parables and epigrams, Jesus was able to convey an ethics of love with extraordinary purity because he believed he was bringing to pass the Kingdom of God through a singular act of moral purification.[47] Jesus' eschatological views were false; his self-sacrifice did not bring about the end of this world in the way he thought it would. Yet, ironically, his belief that the world was ending enabled him to offer the most powerful statement ever made of love as an ideal.

Precisely because Jesus embodies moral perfection in such a high degree, he becomes the focus of Schweitzer's ethical mysticism, both before and after he developed reverence for life as an ethical theory. Schweitzer embraces 'Jesus mysticism', a moral mysticism that is distinct from other-worldly 'Christ mysticism' based on theological dogmas, according to which we become united with Jesus 'in the knowledge of a shared [ethical] aspiration, when we feel that our will is clarified, enriched and enlivened by his will and when we rediscover ourselves through him'.[48] Our lives are illuminated through the love espoused by Jesus, an ideal love in which we relate to each other in a spirit of genuine caring and locate our good in relationships of love. Reverence for life is the love of Jesus widened to apply to all life.[49]

### Love and Reverence

Why, then, rely on the word 'reverence' rather than 'love', and how, exactly, are these ideas related? Especially in his popular writings, Schweitzer portrays reverence for life as 'the ethic of love widened into universality. It is the ethic of Jesus, now recognized as a logical consequence of thought.'[50] That is, reverence for life embraces the content of the Sermon on the Mount and other valid expressions of love in world religions, expands the scope of love to include all living organisms, and provides a foundation for it in philosophical reasoning.[51] Even so, the word 'love' does not convey the importance of reasoning, self-realization and other values having great importance to Schweitzer.

Schweitzer confides to Kraus that his popular discussions of love are imprecise and intended to engage a wide audience, as is his use of the word 'God'.[52] In his scholarly writings, he is reluctant to rely on the word 'love' because of its vagueness, not to mention the many colloquial distortions of its meaning (including when 'love of life' simply means having a good time). For example, he tells us that love expresses human solidarity only in a simile, by analogy with sexual love and parent–child love.[53] Again, reverence for life includes reverence for oneself, which centres on authenticity (self-honesty and self-fidelity), whereas this idea is not captured by the notion of self-love.[54] In short, reverence for life names a new moral perspective intended to clarify what genuine spiritual love is.

Of great interest, the 1919 sermon that introduces reverence for life begins by quoting commandments to love God and to love your neighbour as yourself. It then asks what is the intrinsic good and the 'basic ethical attitude' that provides a 'foundation for understanding' Jesus' teachings in modern times. The Christian audience would naturally assume the answer is love, but Schweitzer answers it is reverence for life. Initially he lists love as only one among many Christian virtues that include 'forgiveness, mercy, love', but he quickly elevates love as the primary virtue of the heart.[55] Love is a broad-scoped ideal and virtue encompassing, but not replacing, the many more specific moral ideals and virtues. Even so, its meaning is unclear, and reverence for life provides a framework that unifies its requirements and thereby strengthens its motivational force. Moreover, reverence for life blends reason and love (the heart), where reason is a deep understanding and sensitivity that expands instinctive empathy and engages motivation.[56] Reason's empathy and love's compassion overlap and nourish each other, in ways that enter into the expansion of love to include all life.

What, then, is reverence? It is a mode of valuing something as sacred, rather than as a mere instrumental good to be used freely for our purposes. To revere is to cherish in an enlightened and committed way. Reverence is more emotionally charged than the ordinary attitude of respect. Paul Woodruff says reverence is 'the well-developed capacity to have the feelings of awe, respect, and shame when these are the right feelings to have'.[57] Schweitzer would agree but find this definition incomplete. Although reverence for life involves emotions, it is primarily an active disposition to support and help when we can. It is a desirable 'mental disposition' that penetrates 'observation, reflection and resolutions'.[58]

As a unifying ideal and principle of obligation, reverence for life says we should preserve and promote the development of all life with which we have contact and an opportunity to assist. Regarding animals and plants, development refers to natural processes in which organisms unfold their nature. Regarding humans, the beings we can most influence, development also refers to growth as defined by values – moral values especially, but also non-moral values such as aesthetic appreciation, scientific understanding and athletic excellence.[59] Beyond that, the exact meaning of reverence, and hence of love, depends on what is revered.

Thus, reverence for oneself implies authenticity, which combines self-honesty and self-fidelity.[60] Reverence for other persons implies compassion, gratitude, justice, sharing experiences, and supporting their development – a development we can influence more than with other forms of life.[61] Reverence for (non-human) sentient animals implies compassion for their suffering and a principled stand against killing them except when absolutely necessary. Reverence for plants implies not destroying them thoughtlessly and, when we can, contributing to their survival.[62] Reverence for God is unity with the divine will as shown by active love for others. By extension, reverence for organs and other classical musical instruments can involve trying to rescue and restore them.[63]

Finally, looking ahead, reverence for life provides a unified framework for transforming moral ideals into spiritual ideals, and moral virtues into spiritual virtues. It does so by widening their scope and significance and anchoring them in a sense of life's sacredness. Such transformations, of course, are not unique to Schweitzer. As additional examples, we might think of love in world religions, compassion in Buddhism, justice in Hindu conceptions of karma, and 'courage to be' in Paul Tillich's existentialism. But Schweitzer's dual emphasis on self-realization and the sacredness of life provides a fresh approach. He devotes most attention to virtues central to self-realization, especially authenticity, compassion, gratitude, peace and justice, but also humility, forgiveness, courage, self-control, patience and perseverance.

To conclude, self-realization requires maximum freedom in how we apply moral ideals and how we search for moral excellence, but it also requires developing responsible moral commitments and spiritual convictions. As we have seen, it is not clear exactly which spiritual beliefs Schweitzer claims are required by reverence for life, as distinct from those which emerge from his personal exercise of freedom and reasoning. Whatever his intent, his views about God and metaphysics are perhaps best viewed as expressions of his personal spiritual views in implementing reverence for life, rather than mandatory components of his ethics. With this suggestion in mind, we can explore the primary features of his ethics without being limited by his metaphysics.

## Notes

1 Albert Schweitzer, *Philosophy of Civilization*, trans. C.T. Campion (Amherst, NY: Prometheus Books, 1987), p. 279.
2 Albert Schweitzer, 'The Ethics of Reverence for Life', *Christendom*, 1 (1936): 239.
3 Ibid., p. 227.
4 Schweitzer, *Philosophy of Civilization*, pp. 308–11; Schweitzer, 'The Ethics of Reverence for Life', pp. 227–30; and Albert Schweitzer, *Out of My Life and Thought*, trans. Antje Bultmann Lemke (Baltimore, MD: Johns Hopkins University Press, 1998), pp. 155–8.
5 Schweitzer, 'The Ethics of Reverence for Life', pp. 227–8.
6 Schweitzer, *Philosophy of Civilization*, p. 309; Schweitzer, *Out of My Life and Thought*, p. 156.
7 Robert C. Roberts and W. Jay Wood cite Schweitzer as a paragon of humility, in contrast with what they criticize as the arrogance of Oscar Wilde in daring to rethink Christianity. They fail, however, to take account of Schweitzer's own radical rethinking of Christianity in a manner that is both humble and daring. See Robert C. Roberts and W. Jay Wood, 'Humility and Epistemic Goods', in Michael DePaul and Linda Zagzebski (eds), *Intellectual Virtue* (Oxford: Clarendon, 2003), pp. 257–9.
8 Schweitzer, 'The Ethics of Reverence for Life', p. 229; and Schweitzer, *Philosophy of Civilization*, pp. 294, 314.
9 Schweitzer, 'The Ethics of Reverence for Life', p. 230; and Schweitzer, *Philosophy of Civilization*, p. 313.
10 Schweitzer, *Philosophy of Civilization*, p. 283.
11 Ibid., pp. 224–6.
12 Schweitzer, 'The Ethics of Reverence for Life', pp. 225, 237.
13 Schweitzer, *Philosophy of Civilization*, p. 309.
14 Schweitzer, 'The Ethics of Reverence for Life', p. 230.
15 Schweitzer, *Philosophy of Civilization*, p. 309.
16 Schweitzer, 'The Ethics of Reverence for Life', p. 227.
17 Hence the argument does not commit the so-called 'naturalistic fallacy' in leaping from facts to values. Whether there is such a fallacy, however, has for some time been contested. See Hilary Putnam, *The Collapse of the Fact/Value Dichotomy and Other Essays* (Cambridge, MA: Harvard University Press, 2002).
18 Albert Schweitzer, *A Place for Revelation: Sermons on Reverence for Life*, trans. David Larrimore Holland (New York: Irvington, 1993), p. 7.
19 Schweitzer, 'The Ethics of Reverence for Life', p. 231.
20 Epictetus, *The Handbook* (*The Encheiridion*), trans. Nicholas P. White (Indianapolis, IN: Hackett, 1983), p. 11.
21 Cf. Wade Clark Roof's definition of 'spirituality' in *Spiritual Marketplace: Baby Boomers and the Remaking of American Religion* (Princeton, NJ: Princeton University Press, 1999), p. 35. See also Robert C. Solomon, *Spirituality for the Skeptic: The Thoughtful Love of Life* (New York: Oxford University Press, 2002).
22 Schweitzer, *Philosophy of Civilization*, p. 303.
23 Schweitzer, *Philosophy of Civilization*, p. 79; Albert Schweitzer, *Indian Thought and Its Development*, trans. Mrs Charles E.B. Russell (Gloucester, MA: Peter Smith, 1977), p. 262. For an illuminating discussion of mysticism see Nelson Pike, *Mystic Union* (Ithaca, NY: Cornell University Press, 1992).
24 Schweitzer, *A Place for Revelation*, p. 17.
25 Schweitzer, *Philosophy of Civilization*, pp. 76, 273.
26 Ibid., pp. 76, 107, 273, 316.

27 Ibid., p. 78.
28 Schweitzer, *Indian Thought and Its Development*, p. 263.
29 Schweitzer, *Philosophy of Civilization*, p. 79.
30 Albert Schweitzer, letter to Oskar Kraus on 2 January 1924 (when Schweitzer was 48 years old), in Oskar Kraus, *Albert Schweitzer* (London: Adam and Charles Black, 1944), p. 42.
31 Jackson Lee Ice, *Schweitzer: Prophet of Radical Theology*, (Philadelphia, PA: Westminster Press, 1971), pp. 25, 28.
32 Rhena Schweitzer Miller and Gustav Woytt (eds), *The Albert Schweitzer–Hélène Bresslau Letters, 1902–1912* (Syracuse, NY: Syracuse University Press, 2003), pp. 94–5.
33 Schweitzer, *Indian Thought and Its Development*, p. 260.
34 Schweitzer, *Philosophy of Civilization*, p. 283.
35 Ibid., p. 304. See also p. 76.
36 Kraus, *Albert Schweitzer*, p. 43.
37 Schweitzer, *Philosophy of Civilization*, p. 282; Schweitzer, *Reverence for Life*, p. 115.
38 Ice, *Schweitzer: Prophet of Radical Theology*, pp. 64–5, 106, 114.
39 Schweitzer, *Out of My Life and Thought*, p. 241.
40 Ice, *Schweitzer: Prophet of Radical Theology*, p. 68.
41 Schweitzer, 'The Ethics of Reverence for Life', p. 239.
42 Schweitzer, *Indian Thought and Its Development*, p. 259.
43 Schweitzer, *Philosophy of Civilization*, p. 273.
44 Schweitzer, *Out of My Life and Thought*, p. 204.
45 Cf. Elaine Pagels in *Beyond Belief* (New York: Random House, 2003).
46 Schweitzer, *Out of My Life and Thought*, p. 60.
47 Albert Schweitzer, *The Mystery of the Kingdom of God: The Secret of Jesus' Messiahship and Passion*, trans. Walter Lowrie (Amherst, NY: Prometheus Books, 1985), pp. 53–72. Although Schweitzer's interpretations of the historical Jesus are now challenged, they dominated biblical scholarship for nearly fifty years. See Mark Allan Powell, *Jesus as a Figure in History* (Louisville, KY: Westminster John Knox Press, 1998), pp. 14–24.
48 Albert Schweitzer, *The Quest of the Historical Jesus*, trans. W. Montgomery, J.R. Coates, Susan Cupitt and John Bowden, ed. John Bowden (Minneapolis, MN: Fortress Press, 2001), p. 486. Cf. Norman Cousins, *Albert Schweitzer's Mission: Healing and Peace* (New York: W.W. Norton, 1985), p. 124.
49 Schweitzer, *Out of My Life and Thought*, p. 235.
50 Ibid.
51 Albert Schweitzer, *The Teaching of Reverence for Life*, trans. Richard and Clara Winston (New York: Holt, Rinehart and Winston, 1965), p. 26.
52 Albert Schweitzer, letter to Oskar Kraus on 2 January 1924, quoted in Kraus, *Albert Schweitzer: His Work and His Philosophy*, p. 42.
53 Schweitzer, *Philosophy of Civilization*, p. 311.
54 Albert Schweitzer, 'The Problem of Ethics in the Evolution of Human Thought', in Friends of Albert Schweitzer (eds), *To Dr Albert Schweitzer: A Festschrift Commemorating His 80th Birthday* (New York: Profile Press, 1955), pp. 139–40. I disagree with Schweitzer here: as a virtue, (proper) self-love does imply authenticity.
55 Schweitzer, *A Place for Revelation*, p. 4.
56 Ibid., p. 7.
57 Paul Woodruff, *Reverence: Renewing a Forgotten Virtue* (New York: Oxford University Press, 2001), p. 8.
58 Albert Schweitzer, *Philosophy of Civilization*, pp. xii, 316.
59 Ibid., p. 331.
60 Ibid., p. 314.

61 Ibid., p. 331.
62 Ibid., p. 310; and Albert Schweitzer, *The Primeval Forest*, trans. C.T. Campion (New York: Pyramid Books, 1961), p. 232.
63 Schweitzer, *Out of My Life and Thought*, p. 75.

# Chapter 3

# Ideals as Guides

> What is the inner connection between the struggle for self-perfecting and action for the common advantage? This is the weighty question of ethics.[1]

The aim of morality is self-realization: 'Ethics is the activity of man directed to secure the inner perfection of his own personality.'[2] At the same time, reverence for life is 'the ethic of love widened into universality'.[3] How, then, is self-realization connected to love and to the common good? This 'weighty question of ethics' concerns moral motivation, which is Schweitzer's primary concern, but it also concerns moral guidance. Does reverence for life provide adequate guidance, or is it too vague to be of much use?

Schweitzer rejects the assumption that ethical theories must provide precise rules such as those of law or even religion (for example, 'pay 10 per cent in tithing'). In his view, ethics is about ideals of character and community that structure self-realization, inspire responsible commitments, and provide at least rough moral guidance. At the same time, reverence for life respects autonomous judgment in interpreting and implementing ideals, as well as in embodying them in virtues and projects of love. Although idealism and individualism stand in tension, and although each mandates flexibility in ethics, reverence for life provides more guidance than first appears.

## Moral Ideals and Projects of Love

Reverence for life is not an amorphous affirmation of all lives that replaces more focused values. Far from being a stand-alone ideal, reverence for life is a composite ideal and an umbrella virtue; it unifies and manifests itself in the full panoply of moral ideals, virtues and other forms of excellence that contribute to self-realization. Each virtue, such as compassion and gratitude, refers to specific aspects of good character that are expressed in desirable actions, desires, emotions, attitudes, activities, reasoning and interpersonal relationships. Ultimately, the justification for each specific virtue and ideal turns on how it contributes to self-realization.

This connection between reverence for life and specific values is made clear, albeit with a metaphor, in the 1919 sermon where Schweitzer first introduces reverence for life. Just as white light unites the colour spectrum, reverence for life unifies specific virtues; and just as white light refracts into colours, reverence for life refracts into specific virtues and their accompanying ideals.[4] Elsewhere we are told that reverence for life fits together the disparate forms of good 'like the pieces of a jigsaw puzzle'.[5] It is the 'fundamental chord' (or symphony) that harmonizes moral demands.[6] It also integrates moral ideals with all other forms of good that contribute to self-realization, including aesthetic appreciation, scientific understanding, professional expertise and athletic excellence. In addition to harmonizing all particular values that contribute to self-development and self-realization, reverence for life provides guidance through these specific values.

In particular, each ideal of character is associated with a virtue that contributes moral guidance. For example, authenticity (sincerity with ourselves) requires us to be honest with ourselves and to develop our talents and interests. Compassion tells us to be caring in response to the suffering and misfortunes of others. Justice enjoins respect for human rights. Gratitude requires giving back in return for benefits received from the benevolence of others. And so forth. To guide our decisions by reverence for life *is* to be guided by all these more specific ideals, as they are unified within an ethics of self-realization and nature-centred spirituality.[7] Accordingly, when Schweitzer discusses what reverence for life implies concerning responsibilities to other persons, he explores specific ideals and virtues such as forgiveness, forbearance, friendliness, compassion, gratitude and justice.[8]

To emphasize, we completely misunderstand Schweitzer if we interpret him as replacing the plethora of values with a simple slogan: Promote the development of life. 'Development' is a normative, value-laden concept. It alludes to all sound moral ideals, as well as additional non-moral ideals such as aesthetic appreciation, scientific understanding, professional expertise and athletic excellence. Whether with regard to self-fulfilment or the progress of civilization, reverence for life provides a framework for appreciating, unifying and extending these specific virtues, but it does not replace them.

Ideals provide only general guidance, however. Each of us must interpret and apply them to the particular circumstances of our lives. We do so, to begin with, by committing ourselves to *projects of love*. These projects or commitments are highly personal, focused and usually discretionary (optional) ways of structuring our relationships and activities in light of moral and other ideals of excellence. Self-realization is structured by personal commitments to friends, family, work, philanthropic organizations and activities we care deeply about.[9] Here Schweitzer takes his lead from Goethe, the thinker who most engaged him.[10] Most of what he says about Goethe expresses his own convictions: 'everyone must realize the love that is peculiar to him.'[11] Again, 'we have to realize the good that is a part of our personal being, thus perfecting our personality, not everyone in the same way, but each as an ethical being in his own right.'[12] And again, each of us has 'a special love' – a particular way to manifest love.[13] By structuring our lives, personal projects set priorities and thereby contribute moral guidance. Thus, for example, numerous moral exigencies emerged to structure Schweitzer's life once he committed himself to his work as a physician in Africa, as discussed below and throughout this book.

Schweitzer often refers to the process of self-realization as self-perfecting. He does not mean, of course, that we can attain perfection. Much less does reverence for life imply neurotic perfectionism, the psychological defence mechanism of obsessing over minutia in order to escape broader anxieties. Rather, self-perfecting is a response to ideals that 'awaken the mind in all of its elementary [elemental] power'.[14] These ideals include both moral and non-moral forms of excellence that contribute to the full and balanced development of our talents and interests (as discussed in Chapter 5).

Reverence for life is a character-centred or virtue-oriented ethical theory that focuses on what it means to be a good person. The theory contrasts in various ways with classical virtue ethics – the ethics of Plato, Aristotle and the Stoics. Plato's preoccupation with the other-worldly Form of the Good leads away from the sacredness in nature, although he deserves praise for linking ethics to mysticism.[15] Aristotle returns us to earth, but he offers a disjointed list of virtues instead of a unified ethic with the power to motivate us today.[16] Stoic ethics is more appealing because it remains focused on practical coping and elemental questions about meaningful life, and it also moves in the direction of valuing animals.[17] Failing to move beyond resignation, however, Stoicism provides no basis for moral optimism – for vigorous commitment to ideals of self-realization and service.[18] In contrast, reverence for life provides a unified, motivating, optimistic ethics of ideals as guides for conduct. Those ideals include faith, hope, love and other spiritual ideals insufficiently appreciated in classical Greek and Roman ethics.

## Ethical Dilemmas and Moral Reasoning

Ethical dilemmas are situations in which two or more moral ideals (or other moral reasons) come into conflict and it is not immediately obvious which has priority. They can also be situations in which one ideal points in different directions. Reverence for life heightens our awareness of ethical dilemmas and it provides some guidance in dealing with them. Unfortunately, Schweitzer sometimes seems eager to downplay this guidance, telling us that how we resolve ethical dilemmas is arbitrary and subjective: 'in ethical conflicts man can arrive only at subjective decisions.'[19] By 'subjective', however, Schweitzer means that ethics requires attention to volition – to motives, emotions and personal commitments.[20] He also means that ethics, as aimed at self-realization, has a highly personal dimension that concerns personal projects of love. And sometimes he intends that individuals must exercise moral autonomy in interpreting and applying moral ideals, allowing wide room for differences among reasonable persons.

Schweitzer's talk of subjectivity must not be misconstrued as moral anarchy, akin to the postmodernist scepticism about moral truth. In fact, as we have seen, Schweitzer takes for granted the objective justification of the myriad specific virtues and ideals. The subjectivity of which he speaks arises within an objective framework of values, as discerned by a combination of enlightened emotion and responsible reason. Although it leaves wide latitude for exercising good judgment in resolving ethical dilemmas, reverence for life also yokes together the myriad moral ideals within a framework of moral objectivity: 'independent thought, provided it is profound, never degenerates into subjectivity' in the sense of irrationality.[21] 'Profound' means honest and responsible decision-making in the spirit of reverence for life. Moreover, we must accept responsibility for our decisions – a requirement that puts pressure on us to think honestly and conscientiously.[22]

Let us comment further on moral ideals as they provide resources for grappling with ethical dilemmas. To begin with, in facing an ethical dilemma we need to struggle against obstacles to responsible decision-making, especially egoism, thoughtlessness, hypocrisy and passive obeisance to societal demands. Reverence for life combats these obstacles by heightening our awareness of how self-realization is shaped and guided by ideals. Faced with conflicting moral reasons, we must 'think out in all directions' the implications of reverence for life.[23] This means taking into account all relevant facts about any possible benefit and harm to all lives affected. It also means thinking through the requirements of all specific ideals relevant to a situation.

To repeat, reverence for life is a white light, a beacon that refracts into the colour spectrum of virtues and ideals, each of which provides practical moral guidance. Acting in the spirit of reverence for life means responding to ethical dilemmas in light of all applicable ideals – compassionate responses to suffering, a desire for peaceful resolution of conflicts, a sense of justice as human rights, a sense of gratitude for those who have helped us, ideals embedded in our personal projects of love, and so on. These ideals structure moral situations and illuminate areas of responsibility and moral opportunity.

Schweitzer insists that no set of rules, neatly ordered in a hierarchy of importance, can remove the need for independent moral reflection.[24] He seeks to overcome the 'fear of what cannot be subjected to rules and regulations'.[25] He sets himself against a 'social morality' of rules which presumes to fully delineate what is morally required of us, including everyday rules like 'Do not lie' and more comprehensive rules as found in traditional ethical theories. Such rules tend to lower moral aspiration to the lowest common denominator, deflating the power of ideals to inspire personal projects of love. There is much to admire in this aspect of Schweitzer's thought. At the same time, his opposition to rules is excessive at times. Rules are not sufficient, but they are often helpful. Moreover, ideals and virtues contain rules, however rough, as part of their content.[26] Indeed, Schweitzer sometimes invokes moral rules, for example the rules 'Do not kill' and 'minimize suffering' which specify part of the content of compassion.

To illustrate how individualism and objectively-defensive ideals interact in ethical dilemmas, consider Schweitzer's service in Africa. Initially, that service was undertaken with his wife, Hélène Bresslau Schweitzer, who was a nurse. Unfortunately, Hélène's health was threatened by the rigours of work in the jungle, especially after she gave birth to their daughter Rhena. Although she returned to Lambaréné for brief periods, and they reunited when Schweitzer periodically returned to Europe, they lived apart during most of his fifty-year mission at Lambaréné. Hélène raised Rhena.

As far as we can tell, the decision is shared, and it is by no means arbitrary. The couple carefully weighed objectively-defensible moral reasons that came into conflict to create a painful dilemma. Those reasons clearly rule out some choices, for example, abandoning both the marriage and the mission. We can assume they undertook serious discussions, even though the discussions are hidden from us, as was much of their very private relationship. Even their closest friends had no clue about the passion in their early romance, which was revealed only after their deaths when Rhena discovered a remarkable set of letters between them.[27] The letters reveal a relationship of intimate friendship that grew into love during ten years prior to their marriage, when it was first consummated. A deep understanding emerged between them that traditional domesticity was not Albert's calling. Initially they planned to sustain their love as each of them pursued an independent life of service, although gradually they came to realize that Lambaréné offered the promise of shared service as a married couple. It came as a tragedy, to both of them, when Hélène's health proved insufficient for work under the harsh jungle conditions.

Judging from Schweitzer's expressions of gratitude to her, Hélène released him to continue the work in which she too was deeply invested. If she had not done so, what might have happened? A divisive and angry divorce would have been devastating, but so would abandonment of the mission they both cherished. There are no rules to dictate the obligatory response to genuine dilemmas of this sort. Both of them accepted responsibility for their decision, and perhaps either choice might warrant some guilt – a topic that bears further discussion in connection with Schweitzer's desire for an 'absolute ethics'.

## Absolute Ideals, Practical Necessity and Guilt

Schweitzer presents reverence for life as an absolute ethics that 'calls for the creating of perfection in this life. It cannot be completely achieved, but that fact does not really matter.'[28] Reverence for life enjoins preserving and promoting life at all times. It requires us to live with a sense of 'responsibility without limit toward all that lives'.[29] Even toward persons we have 'a responsibility so unlimited as to be terrifying'.[30] Can such an ethics do anything but overwhelm us with guilt?

It makes sense to speak of reverence for life as an absolute ideal in that it is comprehensive and encompasses all the more specific ideals which contribute to self-realization, and in that it applies at all times and to all situations in which we make choices. The problem is that Schweitzer often talks as if more specific ideals are themselves absolute in creating not only stringent but exception-less duties (of the sort Kant also endorsed). For example, he says that reverence for life forbids all killing, and that we are guilty each time we kill. Yet he also acknowledges that we must often kill in order to survive. Something is wrong here! Specific ideals cannot be absolute in their requirements if they are constantly conflicting with each other in ways that require exceptions to some of them. Understanding any one specific ideal of goodness – whether compassion or justice or honesty – requires balancing it with other ideals in practical situations.

This balancing and integrating of specific ideals is essential to reverence for life, as to any other ethical theory. Schweitzer fails to account for it adequately, however, because he introduces a confused dichotomy between the ethical (moral absolute) and the necessary (practical necessity). Ethics, he insists, should be pure and exception-less in its demands, rather than mixing 'non-ethical necessity and ethics'.[31] When we look closely, however, it becomes clear that 'necessity' cannot mean non-ethical. He says necessity is the 'unavoidable', but it is not unavoidable in a sense that removes moral choice. For necessity is something we can choose as an option in resolving ethical dilemmas.[32] Furthermore, necessity cannot stand outside the ethical because necessity is infused with moral values essential to reverence for life.[33] Specifically, necessity includes self-preservation: maintaining our existence by eating, self-defence, breathing and walking (which kill microorganisms), and working – for example, the farmer who kills plants to feed cattle, and the businessperson who must fire an unfortunate worker.[34] Necessity also includes self-development, which precludes self-abasement. And necessity includes protecting other innocent life, for example by supporting medical experimentation on animals to develop new therapies, and by selflessly contributing to the lives of some individuals (for example our family) at the expense of not helping others.[35] Clearly, self-preservation, self-development, and defence of innocent life are moral values integral to reverence for life. As understood by his own ethical theory, what Schweitzer calls necessity is part of, not opposed to, the ethical. The ethical–necessity dichotomy is a muddle that impedes his moral reflection.

We can easily modify Schweitzer's account of moral decision-making to restore coherence. In effect, 'necessary' means without sacrificing other moral reasons that have greater importance in the situation; necessity is what is necessary in order to meet more morally pressing ideals. Good moral judgment means finding a reasonable way to balance the conflicting claims emerging from multiple moral ideals, personal projects of self-realization and love, concern for the development of other persons, and caring about the survival of non-human lives. It requires due attention to each applicable moral reason, and attempts to factor them together in a unified judgment about what ought to be done, all things considered. As James Wallace writes, good moral judgment is the ability 'to determine which considerations are really relevant and which of the conflicting considerations are more important. It involves the ability, in other words, to give the considerations the weight they should have.'[36] In addition, we must accept responsibility for our decisions and be willing to give an honest account of how we set priorities.

Sometimes Schweitzer moves in the direction outlined. He writes, 'The fundamental commandment of ethics, then, is that we cause no suffering … unless it is to effect some necessary protection for ourselves.'[37] 'Unless' suggests a morally justified (permissible or obligatory) limitation on the moral requirement not to cause suffering. Here the ethical and the necessary are interwoven, not opposed. For example, injuring an aggressor in self-defence or the defence of innocent parties is ethical, that is, morally permissible and perhaps morally required. Again, he tells us that in each situation we must minimize harm and guilt, a truth that presupposes we can identify reasonable priorities.[38] He also insists that compassion is more basic than not killing, portraying the principle of not-killing as the 'servant of' compassion.[39] All these comments implicitly make 'necessary killing' part of the ethical, not something outside it.

Turn now to the claim that falling short of the ideal of reverence for life makes us guilty. Schweitzer admirably sets a higher standard than conventional morality by linking each virtue to high ideals of love and self-perfecting. For example, ordinary ethics tends to regard forgiveness as a generous gesture which, in practice, flatters us by raising us above the person we forgive. In contrast, reverence for life calls for generous forgiving, motivated by a standard of self-perfecting that forces us to recall how often we have wronged others in the past.[40] Reverence for life also establishes higher standards of benevolence and justice by avoiding cruelty toward humans and animals, maintaining a disposition to kindness, and not sacrificing individuals for organizational goals.[41]

But, we are told, absolute ideals do not merely set a standard higher than convention; they call for perfection. We are ethical only insofar as we promote and avoid injuring life, and we are guilty insofar as we fail to promote life. Here Schweitzer follows the biblical injunction, 'Be ye therefore perfect.'[42] This form of idealism is deeply inspiring to some individuals. For example, Iris Murdoch regards the biblical injunction as a source of inspiration integral to genuine love for what is good.[43] A vision of perfection pushes us to unfold our highest capacities, and it pulls us towards ideals of sympathetic engagement with other life so as to establish wider circles of meaning.[44] This moral push and pull converge around the principle that good consists in preserving and promoting life.

Perhaps for most of us, however, an absolute ethics threatens moral motivation. Schweitzer insists that guilt is not removed simply because we are caught in dilemmas which, of necessity, force us to cause harm whichever choice we make.[45] Because there is always some harm caused in resolving conflicts among values, we must live with guilt: 'the good conscience is an invention of the devil.'[46] The upshot is guilt at every turn, as well as the unending responsibility to repay debts for wrongdoing.[47] Many of us cannot live that way. From Freud on, psychologists have cautioned about the distortions that come from 'perfectionism'. Unrealistic moral aspirations risk crushing us with guilt, and when combined with absolutism it would have us live with a constant sense of being guilty for causing harm to other lives and for failing to promote the good of all lives we encounter. Such absolutism can easily become a source of psychopathology.[48]

The issue is not just about moral psychology, however. It is about moral reasonableness. When we choose immorally, all things considered, we are guilty. But we are not guilty for violating duty simply because we cause some bad and fail to promote good in every possible direction. Neither duty nor ideals forbid all killing and require support for all life; both permit justified killing. In effect, Schweitzer conflates goodness and duty, continuously shifting from 'it is *good* to promote life' to 'we *ought* to promote life', without exception.[49] It is one thing to say we should support the development of all lives as best we can, given our personal needs, projects and resources, but it is quite another to say that supporting other lives is an absolute duty with no exceptions, rendering us culpable for all failures. We can abandon absolutism and understand ideals as embodying but transcending ordinary minimal duties.

Ideals of goodness typically contain a mandatory minimum that specifies duties. For example, ideals of respect for persons imply mandatory standards of justice and compassion. But ideals also enjoin higher aspirations, in particular desirable forms of caring that are supererogatory – desirable though discretionary. Again, the ideal of compassion embodies a standard of minimum decency while delineating additional forms of compassionate helping. There is no sharp line, of course, between duty and supererogatory good works. Nevertheless, there are large domains of goodness where individuals pursue personal projects of love that are admirable but not incumbent on everyone. This revision of absolutism does not mean retreating to an uninspired ethics that places minimal demands on us – we are still working within an ethics of ideals. Nor does it deny that in some tragic dilemmas we can be guilty no matter what we do, as perhaps in Schweitzer's decision to stay in Africa while Hélène raised Rhena in Europe. But we are not guilty at every moment of our lives in killing microorganisms as we breathe, or in killing plants and fish to eat.

## Ethical Idealism versus Utilitarianism

Schweitzer presents reverence for life against the backdrop of an overview of the history of moral philosophy. His discussions of individual thinkers and movements are brief but frequently illuminating, and they contribute to understanding reverence for life.[50] As an illustration having special relevance to contemporary ethics, as well as to understanding his ethics of idealism and self-realization, let us consider his critique of utilitarianism, which centres on how self-interest and altruism are morally related.

Schweitzer groups ethical theories into three categories, according to their starting points and general approach.[51] First, classical Greek and Roman philosophy is largely a self-interested ethics centred on the rational pursuit of pleasure. As such, it fails to move beyond egoism to active devotion to others. Second, philosophy during the modern era (from 1600 to 1900) typically begins by understanding ethics as a set of social rules: either the utilitarian principle of maximizing the general good, or rules about duties and rights. After subordinating the individual to society, it casts about for ways to motivate individuals to care about the general good, but it never fully succeeds. Third, an ethics of self-perfecting surfaces periodically throughout the entire history of philosophy. Bold and venturesome, this 'ethic of personality' (or character) centres on striving for excellence. Reverence for life is such an ethic.

By linking the virtues to ideals of moral excellence, as well as by integrating all forms of good (including what is usually considered non-moral good), Schweitzer develops virtue ethics in the direction of 'inner perfecting', or what ethicists now called moral perfectionism.[52] Moral perfectionism takes many forms, and it constitutes an emphasis (on moral excellence) that many kinds of ethical theory might take. As Stanley Cavell suggests, 'perfectionism … is not a competing theory of the moral life, but something like a dimension or tradition of the moral life that spans the course of Western thought and concerns what used to be called the state of one's soul.'[53] Thus, Schweitzer sets forth reverence for life in a tradition that includes versions of classical virtue ethics (Plato), duty ethics (Kant), religious ethics (Schleiermacher), utilitarianism (Mill in *On Liberty*), American transcendentalism (Emerson, Thoreau) and especially Goethe and Nietzsche.[54]

Schweitzer's version of moral perfectionism begins with authenticity, unfolds in terms of specific virtues and ideals, while emphasizing personal projects of love, and culminates in spiritual unity with all life. Ethics concerns each individual's search for a meaningful life; action for the common good is a manifestation of that search.[55] For the most part, the common good is promoted indirectly, as individuals develop their talents and interests within a framework of moral ideals. The 'great mistake' of most modern ethics was to sacrifice the ethic of personality to the 'ethic of society'.[56] In contrast, an ethics of self-perfecting regards the individual as sacred. Persons are not mere means to maximizing the social good, and hence self-perfecting is more fundamental than a social morality of rules (although they are interwoven).[57] Reverence for life connects self-perfecting to a virtue-oriented ethics rooted in a nature-centred spirituality.

In addition, an ethics of self-perfecting celebrates moral exemplars whose lives provide compelling portraits of moral excellence that inspire and illuminate. References to such exemplars permeate Schweitzer's writings. Most notably, he portrays Jesus as a morally heroic figure who courageously acts on his faith that goodness will triumph evil.[58] Schweitzer also writes books on Goethe, Bach and the apostle Paul, as well as a book on Asian philosophy that focuses on key figures such as the Buddha and Gandhi. The charge that Schweitzer engages in hero worship contains an element of truth, but his concern is to learn from and be inspired by moral exemplars who embody moral ideals.

Like Goethe, Schweitzer sets himself against the impersonal beneficence in utilitarianism. Act-utilitarianism, as it is now called, says that in each situation we ought to choose the action that maximizes the overall good, impartially considering each person affected. Act-utilitarianism elevates moral demands to a responsibility without limits, but it does so impersonally rather than through personal projects of love essential for self-realization. 'Action for the common advantage does not by any means constitute ethics; it is only a manifestation of the struggle for self-perfection' – albeit the highest manifestation.[59]

Act-utilitarianism is flawed in two main ways, in addition to its failure to value non-human life.[60] First, it undermines respect for the individual. In effect, utilitarians treat each of us as mere means to maximizing the general good, thereby reducing self-realization to merely one item to be weighed impartially along with others. In sharp contrast, agreeing with Kant, Schweitzer insists that the dignity of persons forbids treating them as mere resources for impartially maximizing the general good. Human dignity means respecting the freedom and desire to develop projects of love that express our nature. And self-realization requires discretion in how we use our resources, rather than a requirement to distribute them impartially to maximize the general good.

Second, act-utilitarianism fails to provide a realistic account of moral motivation. Most of us are incapable of regularly and impartially maximizing the good of all. A 'social ethics' of this sort is like a tourniquet around a limb; it constricts the flow of blood from the heart of a human being. Our good is most strongly evoked and developed through personal projects of love, as in family, work and philanthropy.

Classical utilitarians made several failed attempts to connect their theory to natural sources of motivation. One attempt begins by assuming psychological egoism, the view that each of us is motivated solely by what we believe is in our self-interest. Next it is claimed that an enlightened view of self-interest connects it to caring about others; for example, our happiness is promoted by reciprocal giving to others. The problem is that this connection exists only as a tendency, not in each instance. Freeloaders might do just as well as or better than altruists in finding happiness. To ensure adequate motivation for promoting the general good, then, social engineering needs to take place at every juncture, from early education to extensive laws and punishment for violating laws. This social engineering, however, destroys naturalness and directness in caring for others.

David Hume makes a more plausible attempt to give utilitarianism a natural foothold by rejecting psychological egoism and affirming an element of altruistic motivation in human nature, mixed with stronger self-interested motives. The aim is to strengthen altruism through appeals to enlightened reason, education and attitudes of approval and disapproval of our actions. Schweitzer applauds this attention to instinctive sympathy, yet he questions whether Hume can make sense of how reason expands and deepens instinctive altruism to encompass non-human life. Hume's dichotomy between passion and reason, which makes reason a passionless faculty for discerning empirical facts and logical truths, leaves no way for this strengthening of altruism to occur. In contrast, for Schweitzer, reason includes elements of feeling and desire that motivate actions.[61]

Schweitzer's critique of utilitarianism anticipates more recent critiques, including the one developed by Bernard Williams.[62] Like Schweitzer, Williams renounces the preoccupation with impersonal rules of obligation set forth by both utilitarians and Kantians. Also like Schweitzer, Williams regards ethics as primarily about character. In turn, character is largely structured by a nexus of personal 'ground projects', or what Schweitzer calls projects of love, that are not incumbent on everyone. These projects include particular loves and friendships, work commitments, and voluntary service to communities, all of which give meaning to our lives and motivate active engagement in the world. We contribute to the good of others through these ground projects, rather than through impersonal calculations of the general good.

Utilitarianism has been developed in new versions since Schweitzer wrote. In particular, rule-utilitarianism says we should live by that set of rules that maximizes the overall good. This approach is less demanding than act-utilitarianism because the rules can be adjusted to make more limited and reasonable demands. Schweitzer would have little interest in this preoccupation with rules, however, for he is convinced that an ethics of virtues and ideals elicits stronger moral commitments that indirectly produce more overall good while respecting individual autonomy. James Rachels outlines a more appealing version of utilitarianism called 'multiple strategies utilitarianism': 'the ultimate end is the general welfare, but diverse strategies may be endorsed as means of achieving that end.'[63] Schweitzer would agree that the overall good is best promoted by affirming myriad personal projects. For example, in discussing the distribution of wealth, Schweitzer says that some people serve society through philanthropy, others through creating companies that provide jobs.[64] At the same time, he insists that the primary importance of these projects lies in self-realization and respect for authenticity.

To conclude, although Schweitzer expresses faith in *reason* in arriving at his ethical theory, he pays too little attention to *reasoning* at the level of practical decision-making. Nevertheless, reverence for life provides moral guidance in terms of specific virtues and ideals, both of which contain some basic rules. Again, Schweitzer's moral absolutism is unrealistic when cast in terms of impractical duties and excessive guilt, but his idealism is inspiring in affirming higher ideals of goodness that we are free to embed in our lives in projects of love. His dichotomy between the ethical and the necessary should be abandoned, for it is clear that what he calls necessity includes moral ideals such as self-defence and self-development. With these adjustments, reverence for life provides an attractive blend of ethical idealism and self-realization.

## Notes

1 Albert Schweitzer, *Philosophy of Civilization*, trans. C.T. Campion (Amherst, NY: Prometheus Press, 1987), p. 164.
2 Ibid., p. 57.
3 Albert Schweitzer, *Out of My Life and Thought*, trans. Antje Bultmann Lemke (Baltimore, MD: Johns Hopkins University Press, 1998), p. 235.
4 Albert Schweitzer, *A Place for Revelation*, trans. David Larrimore Holland (New York: Irvington, 1993), p. 4. Cf. Albert Schweitzer, *The Teaching of Reverence for Life*, trans. Richard and Clara Winston (New York: Holt, Rinehart and Winston, 1965), p. 41.
5 Schweitzer, *Philosophy of Civilization*, p. 310.
6 Ibid., p. 105.
7 On ideals as providing guidance, see Nicholas Rescher, *Ethical Idealism* (Berkeley, CA: University of California Press, 1987). See also Alasdair MacIntyre, *After Virtue*, 2nd edn (Notre Dame, IN: University of Notre Dame Press, 1984); Iris Murdoch, *The Sovereignty of Good* (London: Ark Paperbacks, 1985); and Edmund L. Pincoffs, *Quandaries and Virtues* (Lawrence, KS: University Press of Kansas, 1986).
8 Albert Schweitzer, *Philosophy of Civilization*, pp. 311, 314–15, 328.
9 Cf. Harry G. Frankfurt, *The Reasons of Love* (Princeton, NJ: Princeton University Press, 2004).
10 Albert Schweitzer, *Goethe: Five Studies*, trans. Charles R. Joy (Boston, MA: Beacon Press, 1961), p. 3.
11 Ibid., p. 140.
12 Ibid., pp. 139–40.
13 Ibid., p. 141.
14 Schweitzer, *A Place for Revelation*, p. 48.
15 Schweitzer, *Philosophy of Civilization*, p. 122.
16 Ibid., pp. 105, 124. Schweitzer fails to appreciate Aristotle's unification of the virtues under his conception of eudaemonia (well-being, happiness).
17 Schweitzer, *Philosophy of Civilization*, p. 133.
18 Ibid., p. 140.
19 Ibid., p. 317.
20 Ibid., pp. 292, 299.
21 Schweitzer, *Out of My Life and Thought*, p. 227.
22 Schweitzer, *Philosophy of Civilization*, p. 311.
23 Ibid., p. 315.
24 Ibid., p. 320.
25 Ibid., p. 291.
26 Cf. James Rachels, *The Elements of Moral Philosophy*, 4th edn (New York: McGraw-Hill, 2003), p. 179.
27 Rhena Schweitzer Miller and Gustav Woytt (eds), *The Albert Schweitzer–Hélène Bresslau Letters, 1902–1912* (Syracuse, NY: Syracuse University Press, 2003); and James Brabazon, *Albert Schweitzer: A Biography*, 2nd edn (Syracuse, NY: Syracuse University Press), pp. 142–63.
28 Albert Schweitzer, 'The Ethics of Reverence for Life', *Christendom*, 1 (1936): 232.

29 Schweitzer, *Philosophy of Civilization*, p. 311.
30 Ibid., p. 320.
31 Ibid., p. 317.
32 Ibid., p. 318.
33 Cf. John Kleinig, *Valuing Life* (Princeton, NJ: Princeton University Press, 1991), p. 54.
34 Schweitzer, *Philosophy of Civilization*, pp. 318, 324. Another example is the farmer who must kill some new-born animals in order to keep only those that can be fed and will bring a profit. Albert Schweitzer, 'The Problem of Ethics in the Evolution of Human Thought', in Friends of Albert Schweitzer (eds), *To Dr Albert Schweitzer: A Festschrift Commemorating His 80th Birthday* (New York: Profile Press, 1955), pp. 136–7.
35 Schweitzer, *Philosophy of Civilization*, pp. 318, 325.
36 James D. Wallace, *Moral Relevance and Moral Conflict* (Ithaca, NY: Cornell University Press, 1988), p. 78.
37 Schweitzer, *Philosophy of Civilization*, p. 260.
38 Ibid., p. 325.
39 Albert Schweitzer, *Indian Thought and Its Development*, trans. Mrs Charles E.B. Russell (Gloucester, MA: Peter Smith, 1977), p. 84.
40 Schweitzer, *Philosophy of Civilization*, pp. 314–15.
41 Ibid., pp. 321, 326, 328.
42 Mark 5:48.
43 Murdoch, *The Sovereignty of Good*, p. 62.
44 Robert Nozick uses the language of moral push and pull in *Philosophical Explanations* (Cambridge, MA: Harvard University Press, 1981), p. 401.
45 Schweitzer, *Philosophy of Civilization*, p. 317.
46 Ibid., p. 318.
47 James Brabazon notes that the German word for guilt, *Schuld*, is also the word for debt, and he suggests that owing a debt is closer to what Schweitzer means than being guilty. (Brabazon, Albert Schweitzer, p. 61.) I share the view of most translators that Schweitzer intends both connotations.
48 Cf. Sigmund Freud in *Civilization and Its Discontents*, trans. James Strachey (New York: W.W. Norton, 1961); and Friedrich Nietzsche in *On the Genealogy of Morality*, trans. Maudemarie Clark and Alan J. Swensen (Indianapolis, IN: Hackett, 1998).
49 Schweitzer, *A Place for Revelation*, p. 12.
50 Even James Brabazon dismisses Schweitzer's historical overview as 'optional' reading. Albert Schweitzer, p. 276.
51 Schweitzer, *Philosophy of Civilization*, pp. 286–8.
52 Ibid., p. 57.
53 Stanley Cavell, *Conditions Handsome and Unhandsome: The Constitution of Emersonian Perfectionism* (Chicago, IL: University of Chicago Press, 1990), p. 2.
54 Schweitzer, *Philosophy of Civilization*, p. 288.
55 Ibid., p. 162.
56 Ibid., p. 293.
57 Ibid., p. 229.
58 Albert Schweitzer, *The Mystery of the Kingdom of God: The Secret of Jesus' Messiahship and Passion*, trans. Walter Lowrie (Amherst, NY: Prometheus Books, 1985), pp. 72, 174.
59 Schweitzer, *Philosophy of Civilization*, p. 162.
60 Ibid., pp. 150–62, 229, 287, 320.
61 Schweitzer, *A Place for Revelation*, p. 7.

62 Bernard Williams, 'A Critique of Utilitarianism', in J.J.C. Smart and Bernard Williams, *Utilitarianism: For and Against* (New York: Cambridge University Press, 1973); and 'Persons, Character and Morality', in Bernard Williams, *Moral Luck* (Cambridge: Cambridge University Press, 1981), pp. 1–19.
63 Rachels, *The Elements of Moral Philosophy*, p. 198.
64 Schweitzer, *Philosophy of Civilization*, p. 320.

# Chapter 4

# Environmental Ethics

> We realize that all life is valuable and that we are united to all this life. From this knowledge comes our spiritual relationship to the universe.[1]

The environmental movement that began in the 1960s was sparked by Rachel Carson's *Silent Spring*, which she dedicated to Albert Schweitzer.[2] Writing four decades earlier, Schweitzer laid the foundation for an environmental ethics with several engaging themes: unity of life, inherent value of all life, virtue-guided contextual decision-making and personal responsibility.[3] In developing these themes Schweitzer made problematic appeals to anthropomorphism, biotheism, subjectivity and an enlarged sense of guilt, but we show here that his main themes remain coherent without these appeals. Showing that a view is coherent, of course, is not showing it is true. The plausibility of his environmental ethics turns on how well it meshes with many additional moral considerations, including all the ideals and virtues emphasized in reverence for life, to form a satisfying moral perspective.

## Unity of Life

Theories of environmental ethics tend to be either individualistic or holistic. Individualistic theories locate inherent worth in each conscious animal (sentient-centred ethics) or, alternatively, in each living organism (biocentric ethics). Holistic theories (ecocentric ethics) locate inherent worth in communities of life interacting with the inorganic environment (ecosystems), types of life (species) and nature in its entirety. Reverence for life bridges this individualistic–holistic dichotomy by locating worth in both individual organisms and life in its unity.

The holistic, unity-of-life, theme is prominent in the earliest statement of reverence for life in 1919. Schweitzer voices amazement at life as an 'enormous animated chaos of creation' that 'renews itself' in 'infinite, yet ever new, manifestations'.[4] He expresses astonishment at how life arises, passes away and endlessly transforms into other life. And he elicits a sense of unity with all life each time we contribute to another living creature in a spirit of love.

More fully, the unity-of-life theme draws together an array of ideas and experiences that permeate Schweitzer's writings.

1. Plants, animals and humans interact in complex interdependencies of food, energy and death that make possible new life. At every turn, human survival depends on these interdependencies.[5]

2. All organisms are alike in having a will to live, that is, innate tendencies to survive and develop. Today we can add that these tendencies are rooted in variations on a shared DNA code.
3. We have natural inclinations to take an interest in at least some other human and non-human life, to identify with it, and to respond to it with empathy and sympathy. This *biophilia*, as Edward O. Wilson later calls it, provides a basis for ever-widening appreciation of our kinship with other living organisms.[6]
4. Compassion is a natural response to the suffering and misfortune of people and sentient animals. As a mandatory ideal and virtue, it requires humane treatment of animals in food production and medical experiments.[7]
5. Animal experimentation for medical purposes, which has dramatically lessened human suffering, creates a special relationship of 'solidarity' with animals.[8]
6. Competition and killing within the food chain are not the only noteworthy aspects of nature. Equally striking are cooperation and tolerance among various animals and species that have evolved as part of the shared struggle to survive.[9]
7. Just as humans care for their children, most species of animals care for their offspring; some even care for animals outside their kinship groups.[10]
8. We can enter into reciprocal caring relationships of companionship with many different types of animals.[11]
9. Insofar as we remain attuned to nature, we experience awe at the sheer existence of life and amazement at the unity and variety of living creatures.[12]
10. We feel humility when we understand that humanity is but one among millions of life forms, each of which is vulnerable and mortal. From what we can discern scientifically, we are neither the centre of the universe nor its final goal.[13]

Taken together, these facts and experiences foster a sense of spiritual unity with nature, aptly conveyed by the phrase 'reverence for life'. This sense of unity is also expressed, with varying emphases, in the worldviews of Spinoza, Jainism, Buddhism, Hinduism and Native American religions. It also provides a bridge between Christian orthodoxy and naturalistic worldviews in thinking about the environment. Most important for Schweitzer, it grounds an ethics of self-realization in a palpable sense of being part of a community of life – and being at home in the universe.

Although Schweitzer's spiritual beliefs are not pellucid, they veer toward biotheism: the view that all life in its creative aspects constitutes a sacred force – a universal, infinite Will to Live, of which each organism is a part.[14] Is this biotheism a mandatory, defining component of Schweitzer's ethical theory? Reverence for life is primarily an empirical-oriented 'natural ethic' that focuses on nature as we experience it, rather than on a supernatural deity: 'The only reality is the Being which manifests itself in phenomena.'[15] Even more important, reverence for life is an ethics that emphasizes the need for individual reflection, not obeisance to Schweitzer's personal interpretations of the moral and spiritual ideals comprising reverence for life. If our personal convictions lead us to abandon Schweitzer's metaphysics of biotheism, it does not follow that we must abandon his ethics.[16]

J. Claude Evans objects that Schweitzer's optimistic affirmation of the world is thwarted by invoking an infinite Will to Live and by failing to accept death fully as integral to life. Belief in such a Will to Live amounts to valuing only the morally pleasing (creative) aspects of life, in abstraction from their dependency on death: 'Schweitzer's concept of "life" does not refer to life as we know it, to life that by its very nature is intertwined with death.'[17] Evans thinks Schweitzer believes in a noumenal, supernatural deity, which lies beneath and behind the natural world. I disagree, for I interpret the infinite Will to Live as immanent in the world. I concur with Evans, however, that Schweitzer's devotion to the creative aspects of life, in abstraction from its destructive aspects, is at odds with a more ecologically informed affirmation of nature in its entirety.

At the same time, in contrast with Evans, it is more accurate to say that Schweitzer never fully accepts killing, not death, whether by humans or in nature. Sometimes Schweitzer asserts that even 'necessary' killing is outside the ethical, and at other times he implies that necessary killing might be ethical (morally permissible) but still not part of the creative and sacred Will to Live.[18] Again, he avoids saying that killing by non-human animals and plants is integral to life in its sacredness. In these ways, his biotheism clashes with nature as we know it. It also leads him to view much of nature as a horrifying enigma, 'a ghastly drama of will-to-live divided against itself'.[19] Schweitzer wants us to value the cheetah, to promote its survival and development according to its nature, but to do so in abstraction from its defining nature as a predator of gazelle, each of whose survival and development we should also value. In light of contemporary ecological understanding, reverence for life should lead us to emphasize nature's 'sacred balances' that on occasion require killing in order to create life.[20] I believe that reverence for life can be modified in this way while retaining a sense of each life having value.

## Empathy with Individual Lives

Schweitzer widens the circle of moral concern to include each living organism as having 'value in itself', independently of human desires and appraisals.[21] This life-centred ethics rejects human-centred (anthropocentric) ethics, the view that only humans have inherent worth and that non-human life has value only instrumentally to satisfy human needs such as for food and clothing, and perhaps also symbolic value as with the Bald Eagle.[22]

The will-to-live argument provides the primary argument for valuing each organism. As we saw in Chapter 2, that argument appeals to a combination of reason and empathy to expand our innate but limited sympathy. The more we affirm our will to live while appreciating how other organisms also struggle to survive and develop, the more we experience a sense of kinship with other life. Indeed, we come to see ourselves in other lives: 'Wherever you see life – that is you!'[23] This reasoned expansion of natural empathy renders our attitudes towards all life 'of a piece with' attitudes towards ourselves. Acting in this spirit, our individual acts of helping other living organisms elicits a sense of moral and spiritual unity with all life. Such is ethical mysticism.

The will-to-live argument centres on empathy for other lives, nonhuman as well as human. This idea of *bioempathy* is prominent in much contemporary environmental ethics, and Schweitzer deserves great credit for making it integral to reverence for life.[24] At the same time, Schweitzer is widely criticized for anthropomorphism (even as he renounces anthropocentrism), in personifying non-human organisms as literally possessing human qualities. Specifically, he shifts from (a) 'will to live' in the minimal sense of tendencies to survive and develop to (b) 'will to live' in the robust sense of having intentions, purposes, values and conscious experiences. He tells us that all life 'longs for fullness and development as deeply as I do myself'.[25] Again, 'as in my own will-to-live there is a longing for wider life and for … pleasure, with dread of annihilation … which we call pain; so is it also in the will-to-live all around me.'[26] All organisms suffer, a beetle is capable of 'rejoicing in the sun like you', and each organism 'strives' to achieve its highest perfection.[27]

The obvious objection is that most organisms do not have intentions, desires and emotions like ours.[28] By definition, non-sentient creatures do not feel and seek pleasure, or feel and seek to escape pain. Nor do they have desires to survive and develop, insofar as desires presuppose cognitive and perceptual states. Plants and protozoa lack the neurological structures for desiring, believing and acting – something that Schweitzer, as a physician, was well aware of. Even many sentient creatures lack the *self*-consciousness needed to desire self-survival and self-realization. And ascribing a will-to-live to plants and lower animals is anthropomorphic insofar as 'will' implies conscious intentions, desires and beliefs.

In part, Schweitzer's anthropomorphism emerges from his metaphysics. If each organism is part of a universal Will to Live, and if the basic features of that universal will are present or manifested in all living organisms, then anthropomorphism is virtually inevitable, especially if we begin by reflecting on our own will to live. Without this metaphysics, however, there is no basis for literal ascriptions of human properties to plants and protozoa. In Schweitzer's defence, however, I believe he usually employs anthropomorphic images metaphorically to elicit bioempathy, independently of his biotheism.

Schweitzer is a revolutionary. He attempts to radically revise our moral perspective to include all life, and anthropomorphic imagery is a powerful rhetorical tool for that purpose. Even today, the most rigorous scientists rely on anthropomorphic imagery to elicit concern for the natural world when writing books for a general audience rather than technical articles for peers. *If* bioempathy is desirable on independent grounds, then this rhetorical strategy becomes legitimate as a kind of moral poetry aimed at eliciting sympathy and compassion. In fact, nearly all of us do have natural tendencies to experience other life 'in' our own lives, 'feeling as one's own all the circumstances and all the aspirations of the will-to-live'.[29] We can and sometimes do identify with other life at the more elemental level of shared tendencies to survive and develop. These experiences are potentially universal in scope, for bioempathy need not be limited to conscious life forms.

In order for the will-to-live argument to work, however, empathy must naturally tend to widen as we dwell on the similarities of our lives to others. Equally important, it must generate a degree of concern sufficient to develop into sympathy and active caring for the other life. Can we feel sympathy for corn and star fish? In fact, scientists and naturalists do sometimes report such experiences. The Nobel Laureate biologist Barbara McClintock spoke in almost mystical terms of her 'feeling for the organism', including the organism she studied most carefully – corn.[30] Loren Eiseley sympathetically portrays a 'star thrower' who caringly returns a stranded star fish to the ocean.[31] And John Muir, William Wordsworth and a host other naturalists become attuned to the lives of the organisms they study. These experiences, I would add, involve fascination with differences and variety among organisms, in addition to empathy based on similarities and sensed kinship.

What about compassion and sympathy, that is, feelings of active concern beyond empathetic identification? Schweitzer calls for 'compassion towards every living thing'.[32] Yet compassion seems reasonable only towards sentient creatures, not towards plants and lower animals. Is he implying the absurdity that plants feel pain? In his careful moments, he says that each life involves 'something like' sensitivity, which might plausibly be construed as a responsiveness of any kind – conscious or non-conscious – to its environment.[33] Indeed, in places he agrees that compassion is focused on suffering.[34] At the same time, I suggest, he often expands suffering to include all types of misfortune, not just pain. In this way, he expands compassion to include sympathetic responses to misfortunes. This widening is not a radical departure from common sense. For example, we feel compassion for an infant (not just its parents) when we learn that it has been instantaneously killed in a car accident or terrorist explosion, even though the death was not preceded by suffering. We also feel compassion for a family member who is in a coma but not in pain.

Granted, these examples concern creatures capable of suffering. Can we feel compassion and sympathy towards a plant because of its impending misfortune? Schweitzer reports feeling 'compassion for the palm-trees' being engulfed by the jungle.[35] He makes an effort to dig them up and replant them elsewhere, even though they lacked economic value because there are so many of them. He also commiserates with the 'poor palms' that are doomed to die because of over-nesting by weaverbirds, although this time he allows the trees to die for the sake of the weaverbirds.[36] Obviously he cares about the trees, and he is saddened by the prospect of their demise. Again, he is pained by the practice of decorating rooms with cut flowers.[37] If these responses seem extreme, they are by no means bizarre. Many of us care deeply about a cherished orchid or oak tree. Although it is a stretch to move from caring for a plant to compassion in light of its misfortune, we are not dealing with an emotional abyss.

In short, we can make sense of empathy, sympathy and compassion towards non-human lives without relying on objectionable types of anthropomorphizing. Yet, making sense is one thing; justifying is another. Why ought we to cultivate such feelings towards all non-human life? The answer cannot be that all life has value, for that begs the question. The will-to-live argument is designed to show that we ought to feel empathy and compassion because all lives are like us, in a morally relevant way. That way consists in having a will to live, understood as tendencies to survive and develop according to its nature. Even after we set aside anthropomorphic images, however, we can understand most organisms as having these tendencies. Several recent ethicists have contributed to this understanding. For example, Paul Taylor says that each organism is a 'teleological center of life, striving to preserve itself and realize its good in its own unique way'.[38] John Kleinig suggests, 'a characteristic of most, if not all, living things is that they have a *telos* – they are beings whose fulfillment is embodied in a life-cycle.'[39] And Gary E. Varner says, 'all and only individual living organisms have morally considerable interests.'[40]

Ultimately, how far we widen the circle of moral concern turns on our capacities for bioempathy, and those capacities vary greatly. I find myself utterly unable to feel sympathy-generating empathy for microorganisms that threaten human lives. Even when I understand their role within wider ecosystems, I feel no sorrow or regret in eradicating them. Nor, however, do I find myself eager to draw a sharp line that separates valuable from non-valuable life. Within wide limits, Schweitzer's expansion of empathy to ever-widening circles of living organisms is an appealing ideal.

Finally, the will-to-live argument also turns on the assumption that what is most 'elemental' about us is our will to live, our will to survive and develop, which we share with other life. If our will to live is the most elemental basis for our instinctive self-affirmation, then the will-to-live argument remains promising. Its gist is this: we value ourselves because of our will to live; all other life has a will to live which bears significant similarities to our own; therefore we should value all other life, building on our capacities for empathy. But is our will to live the basis for our instinctive self-affirmation? Note that the argument does not say our will to live provides the moral justification for affirming our lives; nor does it say we value our lives primarily because we have a will to live. It simply says that our will to live contains this self-affirmation, and that our will to live, our tendency to survive and develop, is the most elemental basis for self-affirmation. It defines us and our worth in a more elemental way than our capacity for rational thought. This claim seems to me plausible; we do and should value ourselves at this level, a level more basic than respect for our character or even our status as moral agents. At the same time, we rightly value ourselves for many additional reasons that transcend the minimal will to live shared with other life forms. This brings us to the issue of ranking life forms.

## Valuing Species

When Schweitzer first introduced reverence for life he took for granted that human life has greater value than non-human life, in particular that children are more precious than the deadly tuberculosis bacillus that kills them.[41] Only a few years later, however, he renounced general moral rankings of both species and individual lives, and he retained this stance despite widespread criticism. The ethical person, he tells us, 'does not ask how far this or that life deserves one's sympathy as being valuable, nor, beyond that, whether and to what degree it is capable of feeling. Life as such is sacred to him.'[42] Stated more cautiously, there are no 'hard and fast gradations in value between living organisms'.[43]

Does this mean he endorses radical biocentric egalitarianism, according to which each living organism has equal worth with every other organism? Does he believe that 'ethically there is no distinction among' living organisms, as commentators suggest, such that a protozoan and a person have equal ethical significance?[44] Surely not!

Schweitzer emphasizes that although organisms should not be ranked in the abstract, we must of course set priorities in practical contexts. He does not say that all organisms are equal in moral value, whatever that might mean. The difference is subtle but momentous. The following claims must be distinguished: (1) there is no reasonable basis for general moral rankings of life forms; (2) each organism is equal in moral value to every other organism. Paul Taylor, in defending his egalitarian version of biocentrism, does slide from (1) to (2), telling us that all organisms 'have the *same* inherent worth, since none is superior to another'.[45] Schweitzer is far more careful. After all, to assert equal worth would itself be a type of ranking, namely an egalitarian one. When Schweitzer says 'I must regard other life than my own with equal reverence', he is asserting that other life, like myself, is worthy of reverence; he is not commenting on its relative degree of worth.[46]

In his personal conduct, Schweitzer clearly assumes that vital human interests usually have moral priority when they conflict with those of plants and (non-human) animals.[47] Even his beloved pet pelican, when injured, is helped only after care is provided to human patients. Only in a rare emergency is an animal's vital needs given priority over the less urgent needs of human patients.[48] He also assumes that medical experiments on animals are permissible when they promise great benefit to humanity and are performed as humanely as possible.[49] To be sure, the immediate issue is not whether Schweitzer personally sets reasonable priorities; it is whether his ethical theory provides a basis for all reasonable persons to do so. Why renounce rankings?

Schweitzer offers two reasons, each interesting but neither sufficient.[50] First, rankings encourage abuse, callousness and the dismissal of some forms of life as worthless and destroyable at whim. This is a genuine problem, but it can be tackled by exercising good moral judgment. Second, he insists that rankings cannot be justified in terms of differential contributions of life forms to the universe, since we lack knowledge of any such cosmic contributions or roles. In reply, such knowledge is irrelevant. Ethics is about humans having to set priorities based on what we do know. Schweitzer implies as much; it is just that he insists the priorities should be limited to particular situations.

We might agree that rankings should be made only when they have a practical point and justification. Even so, there are many such justifications, including purposes that go beyond individual decisions and bear on public policy and moral community, not to mention sanity. If we are sane and morally competent, we know that persons have greater moral value than protozoa. This moral value is not an abstraction, but instead it is delineated in practical norms about how humans deserve to be treated. The norms, for example, specify that we ought not to experiment on humans without their consent, whereas medical experimentation on even sentient animals can be justified when it saves many human lives. The norms also specify that it is morally permissible to grow and eat plants, whatever disagreements we might have concerning eating meat.

Ultimately, Schweitzer's metaphysics lies behind his refusal to rank human interests above those of 'lower' animals and plants. If each organism is a sacred part of a universal and semi-deified Will to Live, then it becomes blasphemous to grade or rank lives, either as individuals or as members of species. If we set aside the metaphysics, are there perhaps other aspects of reverence for life which justify (permit, require) differential moral responses to life forms, if not 'hard and fast' rankings? I believe there are. And even if we do not fully agree on general rankings, there is a basis for reasoned dialogue about more contextual rankings in matters of social policy, not just personal decisions.

Each life is a will-to-live, a more or less unified set of tendencies to survive and develop. Yet organisms differ enormously in their patterns of development and in their morally-significant capacities. Although we value ourselves and other humans for having tendencies to live and develop, we value humans for additional reasons beyond those tendencies. Or rather, we value persons for reasons connected with the particular nature of their developmental capacities. We affirm ourselves and other humans at many levels, including generic properties (general human capacities) and specific characteristics (interests, accomplishments, relationships, virtues, and so on). At these levels, humans are not comparable to all other lives (such as worms or wheat), and our full worth turns on much more than the instinctive drives we share with all life.

One morally-relevant capacity is the capacity to feel pain and pleasure. In his discussions of compassion, Schweitzer takes for granted that sentient creatures have a moral status unlike that of plants and non-sentient animals. He condemns killing sentient creatures for pleasure, as in bullfighting, cockfighting and hunting for sport.[51] And he condemns the misuse of sentient animals in medical experiments and in teaching science, arguing that experimentation must be limited to the absolutely essential, while minimizing the pain inflicted.[52] He adds that it is more compassionate to kill mercifully than to permit a slow and painful death of domestic animals we can no longer care for.[53] No similar pronouncements are made about experiments on plants. Even if we avoid saying sentient animals have greater inherent worth than other animals, the implication remains that sentient animals make special moral claims on us. Other humans, with their far richer moral capacities, place even greater claims on us.

Conversely, depending on the organism, there are striking dissimilarities in the developmental capacities (as with plants and microorganisms), or striking similarities (as with the great apes). Rarely will the dissimilarities justify deliberate eradication of a species (as they do with the polio and AIDS viruses), but they will justify the commonsense conviction that humans have vastly greater inherent worth than algae. They will also justify cherishing chimpanzees more highly than chiton, because of the striking differences in their mental and social lives.

In clarifying Schweitzer's position, then, I would not defend his refusal of all general rankings of life. We do need to cherish the special sacredness of human life, as well as to highlight the special worth of sentient creatures. However, his concerns about general rankings provide important cautions. Indeed, general rankings easily become vacuous, once we get beyond basic duties to humans and sentient animals not to inflict unnecessary suffering. Most of us allow thousands of children to die each day while devoting enormous resources to our cherished pet or garden. In practice, even in making life and death decisions most of us do make contextual decisions of the sort Schweitzer emphasizes.

## Responsible Decision-Making

When he insists that moral priorities need to be established contextually, rather than as general rules, Schweitzer adds that the priorities are subjective and arbitrary.[54] Usually he makes such remarks concerning decisions to intervene in nature to save one creature rather than another, for example to save a wounded osprey by killing fish to feed it, but sometimes he leaves the impression that all choices between lives are subjective and arbitrary. To a contemporary ear, this language suggests the choices are not a matter of good judgment and reasoning, but instead a mere matter of our feelings on a given occasion. That implication is not a plausible basis for an environmental ethics, and it goes against Schweitzer's own view of how specific ideals – such as self-respect, compassion and gratitude – provide contextual guidance, along with personal projects of love.

To begin with, Schweitzer tells us that reverence for life forbids killing which is not necessary. Necessary, as argued in Chapter 3, does not mean unavoidable, but rather justifiable (permissible, obligatory) in light of more pressing moral reasons. His paradigms of necessary killing include self-preservation: killing in self-defence, killing to obtain food, and killing in order to earn a legitimate living, as in farming.[55] Necessary killing also includes unavoidable killing during the pursuit of legitimate activities, such as crushing microorganisms while going for a walk. In these instances, reverence for one's own life provides a reasoned justification of killing essential to survival and self-realization. In addition, reverence for other human lives sometimes justifies killing. Examples include justifiable sacrifice of animals in medical experiments that save many human lives, not to mention killing dangerous microorganisms to make an operation safe for a human patient.

Another virtue, compassion, applies to both humans and sentient animals. Granted, Schweitzer expands compassion to include caring responses to all misfortunes of other lives, but among misfortunes he gives special significance to pain. He does so in expressing deep concern to minimize animal suffering during medical experiments on them, and also in the idea of a community of suffering (discussed in Chapter 6). Compassion requires supporting sentient life, but it can also require ending it: 'In many ways it may happen that by slavish adherence to the commandment not to kill compassion is less served than by breaking it. When the suffering of a living creature cannot be alleviated, it is more ethical to end its life by killing it mercifully than it is to stand aloof.'[56]

Does compassion mandate vegetarianism? Schweitzer's refusal to make differential judgments about sentient and non-sentient species obscures the urgency of this question. It is noteworthy that Schweitzer became a vegetarian only towards the end of his life, nearly four decades after he set forth his ethics of reverence for life.[57] If cows and cabbages are equally sacred, why should eating the one raise greater moral qualms than eating the other? Once we recognize moral differences between sentient and non-sentient life, especially as we attend to the suffering inflicted on sentient creatures in modern meat production, the issue becomes important within an ethics of reverence for life.

Responsible decisions about eating meat depend on motives and intentions, as well as on situational factors about meat production. In particular, are animals raised and killed in humane ways? Schweitzer forced himself to be present when animals were slaughtered to ensure that suffering was minimized. If we eat meat, we should at least be willing to do what we can to support humane practices. If we can afford it, presumably we should choose free-range chickens and other farm products that allow animals a normal life. Again, Schweitzer tells us that reverence for life forbids hunting for amusement and sport, but it does not forbid killing for food and other necessities.[58]

Gratitude is another guide. We should feel gratitude regarding the animals used in experiments that benefit us.[59] If gratitude is too strong a word, given that animals do not act from benevolence on our behalf, at least we owe appreciation. Their suffering creates a relation of solidarity with them. Schweitzer thinks of the appreciation to be shown as aimed at all life, but perhaps we can also think of it as targeting members of species to whom special restitution is owed, taking into account ecological factors such as endangered species and habitats.

Peace loving, like gratitude, returns us to holistic concerns. Reverence for life implies maintaining peace with it, wherever possible, and that requires actions that support other lives. We have desires to feel at home in the universe by connecting in sympathetic ways with nature. Additional wide-scoped virtues include humility and, most comprehensive of all, reverence for life in its entirety.

What about Schweitzer's decision to rescue a young osprey by killing small fish to feed it?[60] On another occasion, he chose to shoot some hawks that were eating fledgling weaverbirds, to the audible distress of their parents and the felt distress of Schweitzer.[61] Both decisions, he says, were arbitrary. In fact, the choice to save the osprey might be backed by good reasons, for example, its rarity compared to the abundance of fish, or (today) its protection as an endangered species. As for shooting the hawks, that decision might be challenged on similar grounds. And even if we share Schweitzer's hesitation to make abstract rankings of life forms, we can understand his stories about saving one animal by sacrificing others as parables of good judgment in making decisions about 'necessary' killing.

In addition to generic ideals, our individual projects of love provide contextual guidance. When we form (morally permissible) special attachments to particular animal companions, to particular species of animals or plants, or to particular ecosystems, those attachments significantly structure moral requirements in particular situations.

Finally, Schweitzer says his ethics makes absolute demands that render us guilty each time we kill: 'Whenever I in any way sacrifice or injure life, I am not within the sphere of the ethical, but I become guilty, whether it be egoistically guilty for the sake of maintaining my own existence or welfare, or unegoistically guilty for the sake of maintaining a greater number of other existences or their welfare.'[62] We are 'murderers' when we kill a mosquito and 'mass murderers' when we kill bacteria.[63] These are extraordinary claims! Admittedly, they have a certain authenticity insofar as they flow from his metaphysics.[64] If each organism is sacred, then killing it is tantamount to desecrating the sacred. But consistency is one thing; reasonableness is another. And the reasonableness concerns moral motivation as well as judgments about the worth of each microbe. Schweitzer places enormous pressure on himself and seems to find his feelings of guilt a helpful source of motivation.[65] Most of us, however, would be crushed by comparable feelings of guilt, assuming we could take seriously Schweitzer's extreme beliefs about guilt.

We can respond to a call for greater responsibility for life without being drawn into excessive guilt. In its core meaning, responsibility means accepting our obligations, striving to meet them, and being morally accountable for doing so, that is, susceptible to being called to account for our conduct in terms of good moral reasons.[66] When those reasons are sound and sufficient, killing is justified and guilt need not be involved. In particular, there is no guilt – none whatsoever – when a physician kills bacteria by sterilizing surgery instruments or when patients take antibiotics. Nor is there guilt when we eat vegetables and non-sentient animals (leaving aside the controversy over vegetarianism).

It does not follow that we should never feel bad when we kill justifiably. *Regret* and *sadness* are often entirely appropriate. Regret is the appropriate emotion when we reasonably wish we did not have to take life, by contrast with guilt for unjustified killing. Regret can be mild or intense, and it can be accompanied by strong feelings of sadness, grief and horror, as when we must euthanize a beloved pet suffering from a terminal illness. In addition to being focused on specific acts of killing, regret can be a general response to our immersion in the cycle of killing.

If we reassert common sense in justifying 'necessary' killing, have we abandoned the spirit of reverence for life? No. Reverence for life includes reverence for our own lives, as manifested in self-defence. Admirably, Schweitzer wanted to avoid an ethic of expediency in which human concerns automatically override the interests of other life forms. But in doing so he established a misleading dichotomy between the ethical and the necessary. To be consistent, he should say that the ethical includes necessary killing (in self-defence and the defence of other life), not contrasts with it. We can agree that we should be more cognizant of killing, that we should avoid 'thoughtless' killing and accept responsibility for killing – responsibility understood in terms of reasonable standards for responsibilities (obligations) concerning killing. But we should also move away from the kind of excessive guilt that is generated by Schweitzer's metaphysics.

To conclude, Schweitzer's spirituality contributes to the boldness with which he sets forth a nature-centred ethics decades before most philosophers began to struggle with environmental ethics. Although his metaphysical belief in an overarching Will to Live distorts some of his central ideas, the key elements in his ethics survive intact after problematic aspects are set aside. Those key elements include unity of life, empathy for other organisms based on shared instincts, a flexible virtue-guided perspective unified in a spiritual ideal of reverence for life, and responsible commitment to furthering life while being sensitive to differences among life forms. When Schweitzer calls upon us to stop killing thoughtlessly, to think before we kill, he intends that we should think *well* by exercising good moral judgment.

## Notes

1 Albert Schweitzer, 'Religion and Modern Civilization', *Christian Century*, 51 (28 November 1934): 1520.

2 Rachel Carson, *Silent Spring* (Boston, MA: Houghton Mifflin, 1962).

3 Although I disagree with parts of their interpretations, the following philosophers provide insightful discussions of Schweitzer's environmental ethics: J. Baird Callicott, 'On the Intrinsic Value of Nonhuman Species', in Bryan G. Norton (ed.), *The Preservation of the Species: The Value of Biological Diversity* (Princeton, NJ: Princeton University Press, 1986), pp. 153–5; John Kleinig, *Valuing Life* (Princeton, NJ: Princeton University Press, 1991), pp. 47–56; Lawrence E. Johnson, *A Morally Deep World* (New York: Cambridge University Press, 1991), pp. 134–41; Erazim Kohak, *The Green Halo: A Bird's-Eye View of Ecological Ethics* (Chicago, IL: Open Court, 2000), pp. 79–83; J. Claude Evans, *With Respect for Nature* (Albany, NY: State University of New York Press, 2005); and Joseph R. DesJardins, *Environmental Ethics: An Introduction to Environmental Philosophy*, 4th edn (Belmont, CA: Wadsworth, 2006), pp. 131–4. An additional indication of renewed interest in Schweitzer is the inclusion of his writings in several widely used anthologies, such as Tom Regan and Peter Singer (eds), *Animal Rights and Human Obligations*, 2nd edn (Englewood Cliffs, NJ: Prentice Hall, 1989); Susan J. Armstrong and Richard G. Botzler (eds), *Environmental Ethics* (New York: McGraw-Hill, 1993); Louis P. Pojman (ed.), *Environmental Ethics: Readings in Theory and Application* (Boston, MA: Jones and Bartlett, 1994).

4 Albert Schweitzer, *A Place for Revelation*, trans. David Larrimore Holland (New York: Irvington, 1993), p. 10.

5 Albert Schweitzer, 'The Ethics of Reverence for Life', *Christendom*, 1 (1936): 237.

6 Ibid., p. 225. See also Edward O. Wilson, *Biophilia* (Cambridge, MA: Harvard University Press, 1984), pp. 1, 85.

7 Albert Schweitzer, *Philosophy of Civilization*, trans. C.T. Campion (Amherst, NY: Prometheus Books, 1987), p. 318.

8 Ibid.

9 Ibid., p. 260.

10 Schweitzer, 'The Ethics of Reverence for Life', pp. 237–9; Schweitzer, *Philosophy of Civilization*, pp. 224–6.

11 Albert Schweitzer, *Letters, 1905–1965*, trans. Joachim Neugroschel, ed. Hans Walter Bahr (New York: Macmillan, 1992), p. 350.

12 Albert Schweitzer, *Reverence for Life: Sermons 1909–1919*, trans. Reginald H. Fuller (New York: Irvington, 1993), pp. 114–15.

13 Schweitzer, 'The Ethics of Reverence for Life', p. 226; Schweitzer, 'Religion and Modern Civilization', p. 1520.

14 Schweitzer, *Philosophy of Civilization*, p. 283; cf. p. 79. In this regard, Schweitzer is influenced by Schopenhauer's voluntarist metaphysics according to which ultimate reality is will. Schopenhauer's influence is unmistakable in the rare passages where the entire world (not just life), including inorganic crystals and snowflakes, is said to manifest the will to live (*Philosophy of Civilization*, p. 282; *Reverence for Life*, p. 115). Such passages are ubiquitous in Arthur Schopenhauer, *The World as Will and Representation*, trans. E.F.J. Payne, vol II (New York: Dover Publications, 1966). Unlike Schopenhauer, Schweitzer was deeply religious, and Schweitzer's optimism is polar-opposites to Schopenhauer's thoroughgoing pessimism.

15 Schweitzer, *Philosophy of Civilization*, p. 304; Schweitzer, 'The Ethics of Reverence for Life', p. 235.

16 Cf. James F. Doyle, 'Schweitzer's Extension of Ethics to All Life', *Journal of Value Inquiry*, 11 (1977), p. 45.

17 Evans, *With Respect for Nature*, p. 130. Cf. Kohak, *The Green Halo*, p. 93.

18 Schweitzer, *Philosophy of Civilization*, pp. 309, 317, 324.

19 Ibid., p. 312.

20 David Suzuki, *The Sacred Balance: Rediscovering Our Place in Nature* (Vancouver: Greystone Books, 2002).

21 Schweitzer, *Philosophy of Civilization*, p. 57. The expression 'widening the circle', which Peter Singer popularized, is used by Schweitzer in *Indian Thought and Its Development*, trans. Mrs Charles E.B. Russell (Gloucester, MA: Peter Smith, 1977), p. 251, among other places.

22 On inherent value, see DesJardins, *Environmental Ethics*, p. 112.

23 Schweitzer, *A Place for Revelation*, p. 10.

24 After criticizing Schweitzer, J. Baird Callicott appeals to 'bio-empathy' in 'On the Intrinsic Value of Nonhuman Species', pp. 156–62. My interpretation of Schweitzer brings their views somewhat closer together. Schweitzer-like appeals to empathy can also be found in John A. Fisher, 'Taking Sympathy Seriously: A Defense of Our Moral Psychology Toward Animals', in Eugene C. Hargrove (ed.), *The Animal Rights/Environmental Ethics Debate: The Environmental Perspective* (Albany, NY: State University of New York Press, 1992), pp. 227–48; Kenneth E. Goodpaster, 'On Being Morally Considerable', *The Journal of Philosophy*, 75 (1978): 308–25; and Paul Taylor, *Respect for Nature* (Princeton, NJ: Princeton University Press, 1986).

25 Schweitzer, 'The Ethics of Reverence for Life', p. 230.

26 Schweitzer, *Philosophy of Civilization*, p. 309.

27 Schweitzer, *Letters, 1905–1965*, p. 336; Schweitzer, *Reverence for Life*, p. 115; Schweitzer, *Philosophy of Civilization*, p. 282.

28 Peter Singer, *Writings on an Ethical Life* (New York: HarperCollins, 2000), pp. 99–100; Tom Regan, *The Case for Animal Rights*, updated edn (Berkeley, CA: University of California Press, 2004), pp. 241–3.

29 Schweitzer, *Philosophy of Civilization*, p. 311.

30 Evelyn Fox Keller, *A Feeling for the Organism: The Life and Work of Barbara McClintock* (New York: W.H. Freeman and Company, 1983).

31 Loren Eiseley, *The Star Thrower* (San Diego, CA: Harcourt Brace, 1978), pp. 169–85.

32 Albert Schweitzer, 'The Problem of Ethics in the Evolution of Human Thought', in Friends of Albert Schweitzer (eds), *To Dr Albert Schweitzer: A Festschrift Commemorating His 80th Birthday* (New York: Profile Press, 1955), p. 137. See also Schweitzer, *A Place for Revelation*, p. 11.

33 Schweitzer, *A Place for Revelation*, p. 25.

34 Schweitzer, *Philosophy of Civilization*, p. 311.

35 Albert Schweitzer, *The Primeval Forest*, trans. C.T. Campion (New York: Pyramid Books, 1961), p. 232.

36 Schweitzer, *Letters, 1905–1965*, p. 303.

37 Schweitzer, *A Place for Revelation*, p. 27.

38 Taylor, *Respect for Nature*, p. 121.

39 Kleinig, *Valuing Life*, p. 172.

40 Gary E. Varner, *In Nature's Interests?: Interests, Animal Rights, and Environmental Ethics* (New York: Oxford University Press, 1998), p. 7.

41 Schweitzer, *A Place for Revelation*, pp. 15–16; cf. p. 26.

42 Schweitzer, *Philosophy of Civilization*, p. 310.

43 Albert Schweitzer, *The Teaching of Reverence for Life*, trans. Richard and Clara Winston (New York: Holt, Rinehart and Winston, 1965), p. 47.
44 Kohak, *The Green Halo*, p. 81. See also Mary Anne Warren, who misinterprets Schweitzer in this way in *Moral Status: Obligations to Persons and Other Living Things* (New York: Oxford University Press, 1997), p. 33.
45 Taylor, *Respect for Nature*, p. 155.
46 Schweitzer, 'The Ethics of Reverence for Life', p. 230.
47 James Brabazon, *Albert Schweitzer: A Biography*, 2nd edn (Syracuse, NY: Syracuse University Press, 2000), p. 281.
48 Edgar Berman, *In Africa with Schweitzer* (New York: Harper and Row, 1986), pp. 188–93.
49 Schweitzer, *Philosophy of Civilization*, p. 318.
50 Albert Schweitzer, *Out of My Life and Thought*, trans. Antje Bultmann Lemke (Baltimore, MD: Johns Hopkins University Press, 1998), p. 235; Schweitzer, *The Teaching of Reverence for Life*, p. 47.
51 Schweitzer, *A Place for Revelation*, pp. 27–8. See also Albert Schweitzer, *The Animal World of Albert Schweitzer*, trans. Charles R. Joy (Boston, MA: Beacon Press, 1950).
52 Schweitzer, *Philosophy of Civilization*, p. 318.
53 Schweitzer, *Indian Thought and Its Development*, p. 83.
54 Schweitzer, *Out of My Life and Thought*, p. 236; Schweitzer, 'The Ethics of Reverence for Life', p. 233.
55 Schweitzer, *Philosophy of Civilization*, pp. 316–17; Schweitzer, *A Place for Revelation*, p. 31.
56 Schweitzer, *Indian Thought and Its Development*, p. 83.
57 Brabazon, *Albert Schweitzer*, p. 495. See also Berman, *In Africa With Schweitzer*, pp. 196–7.
58 Schweitzer, *A Place for Revelation*, p. 28.
59 Ibid., p. 34; *Schweitzer, Philosophy of Civilization*, p. 318.
60 Schweitzer, *Out of My Life and Thought*, p. 236.
61 Schweitzer, *A Place for Revelation*, p. 30.
62 Schweitzer, *Philosophy of Civilization*, p. 325.
63 Ibid., pp. 316–17.
64 There is authenticity, as well, in passages like the following: 'By helping an insect when it is in difficulties, I am only attempting to cancel part of man's ever new debt to the animal world.' (Schweitzer, *Philosophy of Civilization*, p. 318.) Without his metaphysics, however, the compensation is at most symbolic.
65 Louise Jilek-Aall, *Working with Dr Schweitzer: Sharing his Reverence for Life* (Blaine, WA: Hancock House, 1990), pp. 189–90.
66 Kleinig, *Valuing Life*, p. 55.

# Chapter 5

# Authenticity: Reverence for Self

Sincerity is the foundation of the life of mind and spirit.[1]

Reverence for life begins with reverence for self, which is a spiritually deepened self-respect that implies a commitment to self-realization.[2] In turn, reverence for self is founded on sincerity, or what today we are more likely to call authenticity. Authenticity has three primary aspects: self-honesty (truthfulness with ourselves), self-fidelity (commitment to full and balanced self-realization) and integrity (moral coherence in living what we profess).[3] This chapter discusses each aspect, then replies to the objection that an ethics of self-perfecting invites self-righteousness.

**Self-Honesty: Schweitzer versus Sartre**

The most familiar conception of authenticity is found in the existentialism of Jean-Paul Sartre, who happens to be Schweitzer's cousin.[4] Sartre connects authenticity with a radically subjective view of ethics, as does much postmodernist culture.[5] For Sartre, authenticity is living in full awareness of our license to make choices in the absence of objectively-defensible values: 'nothing, absolutely nothing, justifies me in adopting this or that particular value, this or that particular scale of values.'[6] In contrast, Schweitzer grounds authenticity in the inherent worth of persons, and connects it with objectively-justified ideals defining self-realization, while allowing wide latitude to interpret those ideals in a spirit of moral good faith. Like Sartre and Nietzsche, Schweitzer speaks of 'creating values'.[7] But whereas they had in mind inventing values, Schweitzer means embedding objectively-defensible ideals in our lives so as to generate valuable new achievements and relationships.

Schweitzer and Sartre agree that self-honesty is essential to authenticity. For Schweitzer, however, self-honesty is being truthful with ourselves around a core of moral integrity, understood in terms of defensible moral ideals. Self-honesty also implies thinking autonomously and deeply about the values, activities and relationships that give life meaning. And it requires avoiding sham and self-deception.[8] *Living* truth, the truth that motivates us by creating a sense of meaning, comes from within, as a personal expression of caring. All honest reflection on life's meaning has value as manifesting moral autonomy, and it increases in value insofar as it implements defensible values.[9]

Autonomy, then, does not mean arbitrariness. Schweitzer does greatly widen the domain of moral discretion, embracing a diversity of moral solutions to ethical dilemmas, but he takes for granted that discretion is to be exercised within a framework of justified ideals. This conception of moral autonomy derives from Kant, but it replaces Kant's abstract duty-oriented formulations with an ideal-oriented ethics rooted in elemental needs and aspirations.[10] As such, reverence for life offers a more vibrant ethics, while ensuring that moral reflection does not slide to subjectivism.

Charles Taylor, who introduced the phrase 'slide to subjectivism', presents a conception of authenticity that has much in common with Schweitzer's.[11] Both thinkers understand authenticity as guiding our lives by justified values. Authenticity also forces us to accept responsibility for our lives and character, while affirming the worth and dignity of individuals.[12] Defensible values, Taylor says, constitute 'horizons of significance' that give lives meaning – objective meaning (value) as well as subjective meaning (a sense of significance). In addition, Schweitzer and Taylor both take their lead from German thinkers like Goethe and Herder who emphasize personal ways of implementing values: 'There is a certain way of being human that is *my* way', and 'being true to myself means being true to my own originality, and that is something only I can articulate and discover.'[13]

Returning to Sartre, there are additional differences to and similarities with Schweitzer. As for differences, Schweitzer's nature-centred spirituality and his gentle agnosticism about the supernatural stand in marked contrast to Sartre's hostility to religion.[14] And whereas Sartre's outlook is born of Second World War despair, Schweitzer's ethics is optimistic in its willing and hoping, if not necessarily in its beliefs.[15] As for similarities, Schweitzer's elemental thinking and Sartre's existentialism are both rooted in lived experience rather than abstract rules. Again, Schweitzer's preoccupation with moral motivation parallels Sartre's preoccupation with commitment. Both seek meaning in the absence of religious dogmas. And both highlight individualism and personal dimensions of morality.

## Self-Fidelity: Full and Balanced Development

Self-fidelity – being true to ourselves – implies commitment to self-realization, to 'the completest possible development' of our faculties by exercising 'the widest possible freedom, material and spiritual'.[16] Self-realization is not to be pursued in a self-absorbed and self-indulgent manner, but rather by connecting our life to ideals of goodness – both moral goodness and non-moral goodness such as found in the arts and sciences. Self-realization implies developing our deepest interests and talents in a full and balanced way, as opportunities permit, around a core of integrity. Doing so creates a robust self capable of making creative moral commitments in the form of projects of love.[17] Ethics is personal: moral vitality comes from highly personal commitments of love whose content cannot be required of everyone. Each of us has a singular moral task in life, a 'special love' for particular individuals and activities that give our lives meaning.[18] This moral task, and the forms of service it makes possible, can be pursued through work, for example by managing a business that provides jobs, as well as through philanthropy, family or any number of other pursuits.[19] When people seek Schweitzer's advice about how best to contribute to others, he urges them to find their own way to self-realization through service.[20]

Schweitzer's life is a remarkable example of full and balanced development centred on special projects of love. His ninety years (1875–1965) combine accomplishments as a philosopher, physician, philanthropist, peace activist, theologian, minister, musician and musicologist. By age eight he was asking precocious questions: Why didn't the gifts of the Three Wise Men make Jesus rich, and how could a mere forty days of rain cover the earth as the story of Noah's Ark claimed?[21] His reasoning led him to reject religious dogmas, but it also enabled him to emerge from childhood with his religious interests intact.[22] He committed the first decade of his adult life to intellectual studies, along with studying music and serving as a pastor. He earned a doctorate in philosophy, then a second doctorate in theology. At age thirty-one he published his most influential book, *The Quest of the Historical Jesus*, which caused an international stir by sympathetically presenting to a wide audience the nineteenth-century theological scholarship overthrowing biblical literalism. By then he was preparing for his work as a jungle doctor by undertaking three years of pre-medical studies, followed by four years of medical school, all the while earning his living as a professor of theology and as an organist. During his fifty years of service at Lambaréné he built two hospitals, each with multiple buildings, and funded them by giving talks and organ recitals. The hospitals provided medical care to tens of thousands of patients, and his work inspired other health professionals to serve with him or create their own hospitals. After receiving the Nobel Peace Prize in 1952, he became an activist for nuclear disarmament.

A multifaceted life is not necessarily a full and balanced life. *Fullness* and *balance*, like *self-development* and *self-realization*, are normative terms that imply due regard for important things, in a manner promoting desirable forms of growth and unity. Does full and balanced development, however, imply maximum variety compatible with coherence? Thinking in this vein, Lewis Mumford celebrates Schweitzer as a genius in the art of living who sustains a 'dynamic equilibrium' among 'the fullest variety in union'.[23] For Mumford, maximum variety is the means to personal growth, rather than its goal, especially in providing resources for responding to unexpected situations. He praises Schweitzer because 'he deliberately reduced the intensive cultivation of any one field, in order to expand the contents and the significance of his life as a whole.'[24]

Mumford's observations require qualification. Rarely did Schweitzer restrict his basic interests. True, at 21 he resolved to develop his interests until he turned 30, at which time he would undertake a life of full-time philanthropic service. That decision, however, was part of a life plan emphasizing service, and by the time he embarked on his life of service he was eager to leave academia. Moreover, it is no accident that the form of service he chose provided him with the opportunity for years of additional studies in science and medicine. In general, he tended to pursue multiple interests simultaneously and in coordination. Furthermore, although Schweitzer agrees that balanced self-development contributes to resourcefulness and creativity, he celebrates it as integral to self-realization rather than a mere means to it.[25]

Excellence is more important than variety, and typically it requires concentration in a few areas. At the same time, excellence requires developing a range of our 'faculties' by pursuing 'comprehensive' tasks that draw on many aspects of a human being. Thus, Schweitzer praises artisans who engage their trade with intelligence, imagination and skill, unlike what is possible for most factory workers in an era of specialization.[26] As this example suggests, full expression of talents can mean concentrating on one multifaceted pursuit. It is good that Einstein was obsessed with physics even though it required leaving his talents as a violinist at a mediocre level. And although Charles Darwin regretted leaving his interests in poetry undeveloped, the depth of his contributions to biology more than justified the trade-off.[27] Schweitzer celebrates the pursuit of excellence in all endeavours that contribute to self-realization and social progress, including science, art, humanities, business, professions, sports and philanthropy. In all these areas, moral and non-moral values intertwine.

In pursuing self-realization, should choices be guided by what is most valuable or by what we care about most, as shown in what motivates us most strongly? These things can differ: degrees of value and strength of motivation are not identical. Sometimes we desire what is not desirable, and what is desirable fails to motivate us, whether due to apathy, cowardice, lust, greed or any number of competing interests.[28] More important, frequently we care more deeply about activities and relationships which are desirable, but which might produce less overall good than other activities and relationships. Our family and local community, for example, are often much more important to us than the international community where we might produce more overall good by sharing our resources with impoverished families. We should think globally as well as locally, but our personal commitments of love are legitimately shaped by what we care about most deeply, on a foundation of moral integrity.

Pushed hard enough, the contrast between greatest value and strongest caring generates different conceptions of self-fulfilment. Alan Gewirth dubs them capacity fulfilment and aspirational fulfilment.[29] Capacity fulfilment consists in developing the best in us, as assessed in terms of objective values. Aspirational fulfilment consists in satisfying our deepest and strongest desires, what we care about most deeply. What, then, is the 'self' to be realized, given that each of us is confronted with multiple paths of self-development?

For Schweitzer, it is a self characterized by moral excellence in accord with the core values of reverence for life. It is also a self that we can affirm, indeed love, in a manner that generates optimism and self-affirmation.[30] For Schweitzer, both excellence and motivation matter – both capacity and aspiration fulfilment. Our task is to maintain a confluence of ethics, excellence and happiness. Even so, there is usually more than one desirable self configured by our talents, opportunities and the values of reverence for life. Choosing among these possible selves requires self-honesty and integrity. Here, as elsewhere, authenticity has a fundamental importance in shaping our lives.

## Integrity: My Life is My Argument

'My life is my argument', Schweitzer tells us, and he challenges each of us to live in a manner that can justify a similar statement. This idea flows from his commitment to unifying thought and conduct.[31] No material reward is worth the cost of betraying fundamental convictions through self-indulgence or hypocrisy.[32] Integrity also implies appreciating the good inherent in our nature that can be translated into practical commitments and personal projects of love.[33] Beyond maintaining integrity, however, it is not immediately clear how a life can be an argument. A life establishes that an idea or value can be lived, and that a particular individual is capable of living it. But how can a life be an argument in the sense of establishing a truth or justifying a value?

The most famous occasion on which Schweitzer says his life is his argument is when Norman Cousins asks him whether he is glad he went to Africa.[34] He replies that he is very glad, in part because it led to his conception of reverence for life, and in part because it enabled him to make his life his argument. The relevant argument is not for reverence for life, of course, since that idea comes later. Instead, it is an argument for views he published before going to Africa. These earlier views were his controversial religious and theological views, for example his agnosticism about a supernatural deity, and his contention that Jesus held the false (empirical) belief that the world would end during his lifetime. These convictions confronted Schweitzer with a dilemma: teach what he believes, which would cause 'painful controversy' among the community of conventional believers, including his family (his father was a Lutheran minister); or teach what he does not believe, which would be dishonest. Refusing both options, he chose to put his beliefs about ethics into practice through direct service at Lambaréné: 'I would advocate the things I believed in terms of the life I lived and what I did.'[35] In this context, then, argument means advocacy. Advocacy differs from justification, in the sense of giving reasons for a belief or value. What a person advocates might be false and unjustified, in part or in total. Our lives and actions show what we believe in, not what is true; what we care about, not what is worth caring about; what most strongly motivates us, not what ought to motivate us. Whether in actions or words, values remain open to assessment by argument (reasoning).

Perhaps, however, advocacy does bear on justification in limited ways. Justifying an ethical perspective includes showing that it is psychologically realistic in motivating moral commitment. Moreover, a life can teach, caution, guide and inspire. It might clarify and demonstrate ways to translate ideas and ideals into action. It can display new possibilities and show what is realistic or impractical. It can reveal the consequences of pursuing good or harmful ideals in particular situations. And it can show the peace and joy in a life of service. Schweitzer's life does all these things, and hence it illustrates how lived-advocacy pertains to justification.

For similar reasons, a life can manifest harm caused by a thinker's false ideas and distorted values, and thereby contribute to refuting them. To be sure, no one lives up to their ideals fully, including Schweitzer. He places great burdens on his family, in effect becoming an absentee father by leaving to his wife the responsibility of raising their daughter. He participates in a colonialist system, and he is authoritarian in how he runs his hospital. Seeing these limitations writ large in his life helps identify some trouble spots in his personal outlook, as distinct from the overall direction of reverence for life. In short, a life can be relevant to assessing a moral perspective, although the assessment is not altogether straightforward.

It should be noted that interest in Schweitzer's remarkable life has overshadowed his writings, especially his philosophical writings. Mumford largely dismisses Schweitzer's philosophy, telling us that his life reveals much deeper insight than his philosophical writings.[36] Even James Brabazon, author of the finest biography of Schweitzer, advises that most of *The Philosophy of Civilization* is optional reading because 'the real experimental checks on the theory are to be found not in the writings but in the rest of his life'.[37] Schweitzer would disagree. When asked about his beliefs he replied, 'Read my books!' – the place where his ideas are most carefully set forth.[38] In valuing the unity of life and thought, he never intended the one to replace the other.

**Self-Realization versus Self-Righteousness**

John Dewey warned against 'spiritual egotism' in which individuals become 'preoccupied with the state of their character, concerned for the purity of their motives and goodness of their souls'.[39] Such egotism can lead to the most 'corrosive inhumanity' and selfishness, or perhaps to 'morbid discontent' with one's surroundings and 'futile withdrawal into an inner world'. Schweitzer, too, warns, 'in each of us there lives an actor who accompanies us throughout our lives and who longs for good roles to play. … The loveliest role, that which he likes to play best, is magnanimity.'[40] Our desire to appear magnanimous and otherwise virtuous before ourselves, as well as before others, easily grows excessive in ways that turn service to others into self-absorption.

Nevertheless, Schweitzer has been criticized for spiritual egoism, in both his life and his thought. Few would question that he did enormous good, but his severest critics interpret his conduct as manifesting self-righteous preoccupation with his own character and goodness, rather than genuine concern for others. A character in one of Toni Morrison's novels says that Schweitzer 'didn't care anything about those Africans. They could have been rats. He was in a laboratory testing *himself*.'[41] Such claims are unfair. Schweitzer had his flaws, but his concern for the people he helped was genuine and profound.

More worrisome is the charge that his ethical theory of self-realization invites self-righteousness. Even Henry Clark, a sympathetic Schweitzer scholar, warns that his ethic of self-perfecting easily distorts personal conduct: 'a man's nobility and vision are woefully restricted in scope if excessive preoccupation with his own "self-perfecting" distracts his attention from the needs of the fellow creatures to whom he is devoting himself.'[42] 'True ethics must be *goal-directed*', Clark insightfully continues, and 'the goal of helping the needy neighbor in the ditch must always be the primary consideration, not the effect that helping him will or will not have on the Samaritan who is presented with an opportunity to help.'[43]

One passage in particular seems to offer a basis for Clark's criticisms. Schweitzer says that conventional ethics urges us to forgive and help others from altruism (sympathy, caring), but reverence for life enjoins us to do so from motives of self-perfecting: 'It is not from kindness to others that I am gentle, peaceable, forbearing, and friendly, but because by such behaviour I prove my own profoundest self-realization to be true.'[44] I believe Schweitzer's meaning is better conveyed by saying that kindness and sympathy should not be the *sole* motives for such actions, and that sincerity with oneself should also play a role. Most emphatically, he is not saying that kindness, sympathy and direct caring for others are unimportant.

The context primarily concerns acts of 'forbearance and pardon', rather than all acts of altruism.[45] Forbearance and pardon involve negative judgments about others' actions, such that we must decide whether to blame or forgive. Here especially there is a high risk of insincerity and of power distortions from regarding ourselves as superior. Indeed, in this same context he warns against the 'sweetened triumph' of feeling elevated at the expense of others. He cautions against self-righteousness that humiliates the person we are forgiving. A spirit of forgiveness comes as we acknowledge how flawed our own lives are, and how often we commit the sins we so eagerly condemn in others. Otherwise, forgiveness can become a way to elevate ourselves and humiliate others. In this way, sincerity and honesty with ourselves prepare the way for genuine caring. Far from encouraging spiritual egoism, the very passage warns against it.

As the context also indicates, Schweitzer is suggesting there is a smooth ('imperceptible') progression from self-perfecting to helping others. Far from reducing altruism to self-perfecting, he works toward the conclusion that reverence for self and reverence for others interpenetrate. Caring for others and caring about one's integrity are mutually reinforcing motives. As guides for conduct, they also point in similar directions.

Thus, 'the ethics of sincerity towards oneself passes imperceptibly into that of devotion to others', such that reverence for self and for others 'interpenetrate'.[46] One way this transition occurs is through the reasoned development of instinctive sympathy in personal projects of love. We have natural but limited tendencies to feel empathy, sympathy, compassion, gratitude and simple kindness. At the same time, even these emotions, attitudes and virtues of love are connected with self-perfecting. Who and what we love shapes who we are. In this way, love and concern for others is 'not a surrender of the self, but a manifestation of its expansion'.[47] Love is never selfless in the sense of not involving the self. It is selfless only insofar as it is not distorted by inappropriate elements of selfishness, and identifying those elements requires nuanced and contextual value judgments.

Finally, Schweitzer agrees that ethics should be goal directed, where the goal is instantiating moral ideals and directly supporting other lives, and he shares the concern about self-righteous preening that deflects us from concern for the needs of fellow creatures. Moreover, reverence for life insistently links self-realization to genuine caring about others. Reverence for life is not an ethics of formal, dutiful giving, but instead an ethics of love in which motives of caring matter. He addresses in detail how self-perfecting and self-devotion are connected, in terms of both guidance and motivation.[48]

To conclude, authenticity merges with caring for others in many ways. Regarding forbearance and pardon, remembering our faults contributes to a more generous good will in forgiving and in controlling the excesses of blaming. Regarding compassion and gratitude, there is direct caring for others accompanied by a sense of interconnectedness between their well-being and our own. Authenticity implies awareness of how much we need others, and honesty with ourselves implies affirming our kinship with other life.

## Notes

1 Albert Schweitzer, *Out of My Life and Thought*, trans. Antje Bultmann Lemke (Baltimore, MD: Johns Hopkins University Press, 1998), p. 227.
2 Albert Schweitzer, *A Place for Revelation*, trans. David Larrimore Holland (New York: Irvington, 1993), p. 35.
3 Albert Schweitzer, 'The Ethics of Reverence for Life', *Christendom*, 1 (1936): 230; Schweitzer, *Out of My Life and Thought*, pp. 223–8.
4 Schweitzer's uncle was Sartre's grandfather.
5 Cf. Robert N. Bellah et al., *Habits of the Heart* (Berkeley, CA: University of California Press, 1985).
6 Jean-Paul Sartre, *Being and Nothingness*, trans. Hazel E. Barnes (New York: Washington Square Press, 1966), p. 76.
7 Albert Schweitzer, *Philosophy of Civilization*, trans. C.T. Campion (Amherst, NY: Prometheus Books, 1987), p. 79.
8 Schweitzer, *A Place for Revelation*, p. 42.
9 Schweitzer, *Philosophy of Civilization*, p. 62.
10 Ibid., p. 184; Schweitzer, *Out of My Life and Thought*, p. 227.
11 Charles Taylor, *The Ethics of Authenticity* (Cambridge, MA: Harvard University Press, 1992), pp. 37, 55–69. Like Schweitzer, Taylor has strong interests in religion. See his *Varieties of Religion Today: William James Revisited* (Cambridge, MA: Harvard University Press, 2002).
12 Taylor, *The Ethics of Authenticity*, p. 74.
13 Ibid., pp. 28–9.
14 Albert Schweitzer, *Letters, 1905–1965*, trans. Joachim Neugroschel, ed. Hans Walter Bahr (New York: Macmillan, 1992), p. 266.
15 Schweitzer, *Out of My Life and Thought*, p. 242. Another difference is that whereas Schweitzer explains the absence of authenticity largely in terms of lack of opportunities due to socioeconomic forces (Schweitzer, *Philosophy of Civilization*, p. 20), Sartre (during his existential phase) traces it to cowardice. Jean-Paul Sartre, 'Existentialism Is a Humanism', in Walter Kaufmann (ed.), *Existentialism from Dostoevsky to Sartre* (New York: New American Library, 1975), p. 366. At a personal level, Schweitzer was appalled by Sartre's derogatory characterizations of his family, especially of his grandfather whom Schweitzer deeply respected. Schweitzer, *Letters, 1905–1965*, p. 357; and Sartre, *The Words*, trans. Bernard Frechtman (Greenwich, CT: Fawcett, 1964).
16 Schweitzer, *Philosophy of Civilization*, pp. 334–5. Schweitzer would balk at Susan Wolf's portrayal of moral perfectionism as narrow self-sacrifice or conscientiousness at the expense of broader self-development, in 'Moral Saints', *The Journal of Philosophy*, 79:8 (August 1982): 419–39.
17 Schweitzer, *Philosophy of Civilization*, pp. 13, 334.
18 Ibid., pp. 50, 139–41.
19 Ibid., p. 320.
20 Schweitzer, *Out of My Life and Thought*, p. 88.
21 Albert Schweitzer, *Memoirs of Childhood and Youth*, trans. Kurt Bergel and Alice R. Bergel (Syracuse, NY: Syracuse University Press, 1997), p. 21.
22 Ibid., p. 53.
23 Lewis Mumford, *The Conduct of Life* (New York: Harcourt Brace Jovanovich, 1970), p. 180.
24 Ibid., p. 209, italics removed.
25 Schweitzer, *Philosophy of Civilization*, p. 13.

26 Ibid.
27 For an opposing view, see Thomas Hurka, *Perfectionism* (New York: Oxford University Press, 1993), pp. 95–6.
28 This is why 'The Socratic Paradox' – to know the good is to do it – really is a paradox.
29 Alan Gewirth, *Self-Fulfillment* (Princeton, NJ: Princeton University Press, 1998), pp. 13–14.
30 Schweitzer, *Philosophy of Civilization*, pp. 206, 278. On the importance of caring in connection with desirable forms of self-love, see Harry G. Frankfurt, *The Reasons of Love* (Princeton, NJ: Princeton University Press, 2004), pp. 71–100.
31 Albert Schweitzer, *Goethe: Five Studies*, trans. Charles R. Joy (Boston, MA: Beacon Press), p. 143.
32 Schweitzer, *Philosophy of Civilization*, p. 314.
33 Schweitzer, *Goethe: Five Studies*, p. 50.
34 Norman Cousins, *Albert Schweitzer's Mission* (New York: W.W. Norton, 1985), p. 125. Cf. Edgar Berman, *In Africa With Schweitzer* (New York: Harper and Row, 1989), pp. 38, 106.
35 Cousins, *Albert Schweitzer's Mission*, p. 125.
36 Mumford, *The Conduct of Life*, p. 207.
37 James Brabazon, *Albert Schweitzer: A Biography*, 2nd edn (Syracuse, NY: Syracuse University Press, 2000), p. 276.
38 Henry Clark, *The Ethical Mysticism of Albert Schweitzer* (Boston, MA: Beacon Press, 1962), p. vii.
39 John Dewey, *Human Nature and Conduct* (New York: Modern Library, 1957 [1922]), pp. 8–9.
40 Schweitzer, *A Place for Revelation*, p. 42.
41 Toni Morrison, *Song of Solomon* (New York: New American Library, 1977), p. 157.
42 Henry Clark, *The Ethical Mysticism of Albert Schweitzer*, p. 131.
43 Ibid.
44 Schweitzer, *Philosophy of Civilization*, p. 315.
45 Ibid., p. 314.
46 Ibid., p. 314.
47 Ibid., p. 255.
48 Ibid., p. 164.

# Chapter 6

# Compassion: Community of Suffering

> I have never tried to withdraw myself from this community of suffering. It seemed to me a matter of course that we should all take our share of the burden of pain that lies upon the world.[1]

Suffering cast a shadow over Schweitzer's life.[2] It shaped his life plan, especially his decision to become a physician in order to provide medical care for Africans who had only 'witch doctors' to help them.[3] And it shaped his moral philosophy. Compassion, understood as active caring in response to suffering, lies at the heart of his ethical mysticism – the unity with all life experienced in helping even one life. Compassion prompted two additional ideas: 'the fellowship of those who bear the mark of pain', which exists among persons, and the 'community of suffering', which exists among both human and non-human lives.[4] When the phrase 'reverence for life' first emblazoned Schweitzer's mind he thought not of Jesus or Goethe, both of whom had a profound influence on him, but of the Buddha, 'the originator of the ethic of compassion'.[5]

### A Physician's Compassion

Schweitzer's philosophical emphasis on compassion emerged from the 'way in which the commandment not to kill and torture' worked on him during his childhood.[6] In *Memoirs of Childhood and Youth* he recounts a number of incidents that reveal an early and heightened sensitivity to the suffering of animals.[7] He was 'haunted' for weeks by the sight of an old horse being beaten on the way to the slaughterhouse. He was shocked and shamed by his own cruelty in whipping dogs on two occasions. He abandoned fishing because of the apparent distress of the worm used as bait, let alone of the hooked fish. And he attached spiritual significance to the ringing of church bells at the exact moment when he and a friend were about to attack a flock of birds with slingshots.

His compassion continued throughout his career as a physician, as shown in three examples from people who worked with him. The first example is from Edgar Berman, a surgeon who served at Lambaréné in 1960.[8] Berman recalls an elderly man, perhaps seventy, who arrived at the hospital and begged for help for his 'oldest friend', a dog who had been accidentally shot. The man had rowed for two days against strong river currents because villagers had told him that only Schweitzer could save such a grievously wounded animal. Schweitzer immediately ordered that the emergency room be made ready. When his staff objected to the intrusion on their scheduled (though non-emergency) surgery, he exploded in anger. Priorities were promptly rearranged, but the dog died before surgery could begin. With shoulders bent in sadness, Schweitzer comforted the sobbing man, telling him they did everything possible, and that he respected him for his love for his companion. Upon returning to the operating room to oversee the burial of the animal, Schweitzer learned that the dog's remains had been thrown in the garbage. Furious again, he shouted at a young doctor and his assistants for disrespecting the man and his dog. Berman reports that Schweitzer's behaviour was completely in character, and that he witnessed numerous other instances of his compassion for sick people and injured animals.

A second example comes from Louise Jilek-Aall, a paediatrician who recounts that African patients regarded compassion for people outside their tribe as a sign of weakness.[9] This xenophobia made it difficult to treat members of competing tribes in the hospital's close quarters. Added to that, the Africans found it foolish to treat dying patients, believing that doing so weakens the powers of healers. Jilek-Aall recounts a conversation with Gustave, a long-time African orderly at the Lambaréné hospital. For many years, Gustave was perplexed by Schweitzer's concern for all patients, as well as by his sermons on universal compassion, since cross-tribal caring was sharply at odds with African customs. Then one evening, walking home, he saw a kerosene lamp burning in the hospital. Fearing something amiss, given how few lamps were available, he walked closer and saw Schweitzer lift a patient's head to offer him water. The patient was in the terminal stage of sleeping sickness and was shunned by the witch doctors who sought to avoid damaging their reputations by having a patient die. Gustave saw a 'sorrowful look' on Schweitzer's face that in an instant made him understand the meaning of compassion.

A third illustration concerns mental illness, a topic of great interest to Schweitzer. His dissertation for his medical degree, *The Psychiatric Study of Jesus*, examines and rejects the idea that Jesus was mentally imbalanced because his visions constitute pathological hallucinations, delusions of persecution and megalomania.[10] At Lambaréné Schweitzer adjusted his medical practice to accommodate the witch doctors' 'complementary medicine', both in order to maintain peaceful relations and out of respect for their psychological power in influencing patients. And he did what he could, given the primitive state of psychiatric understanding, to help demented patients who would otherwise be treated inhumanely by their tribes.[11]

One such patient was Mama San Nom ('No Name'), a pygmy woman about fifty years old.[12] Schweitzer had a special rapport with her and they communicated using simple sign language. She was probably demented, in addition to having several physical diseases that included tuberculosis and syphilis. Whenever she visited, usually for just a week or a month, she was permitted to roam freely at the hospital, naked and unkempt. In return, she helped other patients by babysitting or cooking. Patients accepted her, even though she was not a member of their tribes. Schweitzer expressed concern and interest, suggesting she might have something to teach about independence, generosity and transcending tribalism.

Schweitzer's life and thoughts have inspired compassionate service in many other health care professionals.[13] Some create their own hospitals and clinics in impoverished areas of the world. Others try to emulate his ideal of compassionate medical care in an era of increasing commercialization of medicine. To be sure, Schweitzer has been criticized, sometimes justly, for inadequate sanitary conditions and public health measures at his hospital. Yet he has been praised for the innovative 'appropriate medicine' he developed by allowing families to stay with patients for comfort and to preserve tribal traditions.

These three examples illustrate how compassion cannot be encapsulated in simple rules. A general statement like 'Be caring in response to suffering' is less a rule than the expression of an ideal to which we should aspire. The ideal consists in active engagement in alleviating and preventing suffering, in contrast with sentimental emotions. Yet the exact requirements of the ideal must be understood in light of contextual nuances, including the circumstances of the sufferer, our resources and our projects of love. Moreover, compassion as a moral ideal can be understood within wider spiritual frameworks, as discussed next.

## Fellowship of Those Who Bear the Mark of Pain

The role of compassion in promoting human solidarity is expressed as the fellowship of those who bear the mark of pain: 'Those who have learnt by experience what physical pain and bodily anguish mean, belong together all the world over; they are united by a secret bond.'[14] The fellowship focuses on physical pain, but it easily expands to include suffering from mental disorders. It is a bond of reciprocal compassion, together with gratitude for having been helped. In this way, the fellowship reflects the two dominant 'experiences' from Schweitzer's childhood, compassion and gratitude, which melded to shape his life and thought.[15]

The idea of the fellowship was developed in light of his severe illness when he was imprisoned by the French during the First World War as an enemy (German) alien.[16] It is introduced towards the end of *On the Edge of the Primeval Forest*. That discussion is prefaced with an argument that Western societies have a duty to help people living in impoverished societies. One basis for that duty is atonement for the harm caused by colonialism – atonement being the spiritual analogue of secular compensatory justice for injuries. He then asks who will provide the necessary aid until this duty is more widely acknowledged. The providers, he answers, will be individuals who have suffered deeply and been assisted by healers. Their reciprocal giving will be directed to suffering that is both close and far away, for being marked by pain unifies us with all people who suffer.

The fellowship is not an invitation to unhealthy absorption in suffering. Schweitzer calls for active caring, and he cautions against allowing compassion to degenerate into sentimentality. This active caring increases our sense of vulnerability, reinforcing spiritual resignation to the contingency of our lives. Yet the active caring also deepens our appreciation of what is important in life, and strengthens our sense of moral and spiritual community.

Inspired by Schweitzer, Arthur W. Frank develops these themes in *The Wounded Storyteller*.[17] He agrees that being helped when we suffer tends to foster empathy and draw us into a community of reciprocal helping. He then explores how experiences of suffering and caring are expressed in 'illness narratives', which take three forms: restitution, chaos and quest. Restitution narratives centre on faith in recovery: I was once healthy, now I am sick, but soon I will return to health. Chaos narratives centre on futility rather than faith, on a sense that no one is in control of the illness. Quest narratives connect most directly with the fellowship of those who bear the mark of pain. A quest is a journey of discovery and transformation. The self is accepted as vulnerable, dependent and not fully in control, as in chaos narratives, but the faith and hope of restitution narratives is widened to include possibilities of growth that transcend getting better. Indeed, sometimes there is little hope of getting better, and we must simply learn to live with chronic and debilitating illness. Even so, ideally the quest progresses to the stage where we return to live among both the healthy and the suffering. We remain marked by pain, but in a creative way that motivates helping.

## Strengthening Compassion

Many of us who suffer and receive help resist reciprocal responsibilities; we do not enter into the fellowship of those who bear the mark of pain. More generally, most of us find it difficult to remain alive to the ideal of global, spiritual compassion. Schweitzer frequently comments on this difficulty and discusses an array of obstacles to compassionate caring, including egoism, hopelessness, hypocrisy, decorum and the fear that we will suffer in helping others. His comments reflect his concern to strengthen moral motivation by interweaving self-realization and service to others.[18]

'Ignorant egoism' is the primary source of indifference to others' suffering.[19] Infants and young children have innate capacities to respond with compassion, but as we grow older we see the predominance of egoism and cruelty in the struggle for survival.[20] Nature is a gruesome teacher of survival of the fittest, and there is no simple explanation of why violence is ubiquitous in human societies. Although we cannot fully understand cruelty, we should emphasize our own need to lead meaningful lives by showing compassion whenever we can. In traditional religious terms, personal redemption requires compassionate involvement in the lives of others. In terms of ethical mysticism, we experience unity with all life through acts of compassion.

Hopelessness is a second source of inaction, if not indifference. It might take the form of 'compassion fatigue', or it might consist in believing that our contribution is an insignificant drop in the sea of suffering. Indeed, we realize that suffering is inevitable and that in our own lives we also add to the 'melody of pain and death'.[21] Schweitzer reminds us that character and self-realization are at stake, and that the alternative to compassion is callousness. Moreover, the help we offer can have enormous importance for those in desperate need, and there is joy in helping others. Having said that, each of us must struggle to maintain a balance of giving and receiving, largely through the personal projects of love we undertake.

Hypocrisy is a third source of indifference. We deceive ourselves into thinking we are doing all we can or should, and then we proceed with casual indifference to the suffering of others. But 'the good conscience is an invention of the devil'.[22] There is an actor within each of us who enjoys playing the role of the magnanimous giver, while doing far less than is possible in alleviating suffering.[23] We should restrain such self-glorification and do so in ways that liberate valuable passions.

Restrictions imposed by social decorum constitute a fourth source of moral indifference. Writing at a time when these restrictions were far more pronounced, Schweitzer felt deeply torn between the need for decorum in respecting the privacy of individuals, and his moral impulses to break through those restrictions in order to show compassion and caring.[24] He reminds us of occasions when we sense that people need help: a trolley car operator who one day wears an uncharacteristically sad face; an elderly or impaired stranger needing help with their luggage; a neighbour who has lost a job.[25] Although initially we feel hesitant to offer help, overcoming our reticence can 'lift the strangeness' between persons.[26]

A fifth source of indifference has special relevance to the fellowship of those who bear the mark of pain: the worry that compassion adds to our own suffering by immersing us in others' suffering. In response, Schweitzer reminds us that isolation from others' suffering forecloses joy in their well-being.[27] Joy and compassion are inseparable: to love is to be responsive to both the suffering and the happiness of others.[28]

Compassion is not merely a form of suffering. Etymologically, 'com-passion' is 'feeling with', but it does not require suffering in the same way and degree as the person or animal for whom we feel compassion. Granted, sometimes compassionate persons suffer in the same degree as victims or even in a higher degree, as with parents and their seriously injured child. But usually the victim suffers far more. More important, compassion is by no means reducible to suffering in response to suffering. It might be manifested in myriad additional emotions – hope for the recovery of a sick person, joy in seeing a person get better, satisfaction in being able to help and anger at others' callousness (as in the Berman example). As a virtue, compassion is active helping that engages a range of emotions. And compassionate persons do not merely wait for suffering; they actively try to prevent it.[29]

Genuinely helpful compassion is intelligent, not only in its aims but also in its resilience. Specifically, it requires not allowing ourselves to be overwhelmed by others' pain. Thus, surgeons need to maintain professional distance while operating, and nurses cannot be effective if they co-suffer with each patient at the moment of helping. Professional distance can degenerate into indifference, but it remains essential in maintaining compassionate involvement without burnout.[30] With adjustments, similar comments apply to helping in philanthropy and in everyday relationships. Here, perhaps, Schweitzer says too little about the legitimacy of placing limits on how immersed we become in others' suffering. Like other morally heroic and saint-like individuals, Schweitzer was able to live with ultra-sensitivity to suffering that would overwhelm most of us. He reports that his attunement to the suffering around him made it possible 'only at rare moments' to feel 'really glad to be alive'.[31] Most of us cannot live like that; we rely on a stronger need for happiness in coping with the stresses of everyday life.

Additional obstacles to compassion include hatred, envy, ingratitude and immersion in narrowly-defined responsibilities at work.[32] Enough has been said, however, to show that Schweitzer's calls for strengthening compassion are addressed to individuals who are already morally committed in significant degrees. In outline, his argument strategy is straightforward. Why should we cultivate compassion and express it in actions? Because doing so makes us the kinds of persons who, at some deep level, we aspire to be – namely, compassionate and caring. This argument strategy cannot work for everyone, and certainly not for sociopaths. It appeals to people of good will and elicits their natural tendencies of empathy, sympathy, compassion and self-realization. In this way, appeals to good character and self-interest are appropriately connected, reinforcing how altruism and the pursuit of self-realization are interwoven.

Finally, compassion is strengthened by keeping ethical ideals elemental – simple, close to experience, rooted in natural desires, and responsive to needs for meaning. Reverence for life, as an ethics of virtue, highlights how we expand and enrich our identities by relating to others in caring ways.[33] Moral motivation increases as ethics emphasizes personal projects of love and caring in personal relationships, work and ideals of service. These projects define who we are and what we care about most deeply. Inspiration from others, who serve as moral exemplars, is an additional impetus for compassion. So is a widened spirituality of reverence for all living creatures.

## Meaning and the Community of Suffering

The fellowship of those who bear the mark of pain concerns relationships among persons. There is also a 'community of suffering' that includes all life which suffers.[34] We feel compassion for sentient animals as well as for humans, and Schweitzer calls for 'compassion towards every living thing'.[35] As we saw in Chapter 2, this appeal to compassion, along with empathy and sympathy, is the crux of the will-to-live argument used to widen the moral circle to all suffering creatures. And as suggested in Chapter 4, suffering includes all misfortunes, not just pain. This inclusion makes sense of, for example, Schweitzer's compassion towards palm trees about to be engulfed by the jungle. Of course, the cogency of what he says about compassion towards all life turns on a justified value perspective rather than linguistic analysis.

Schweitzer seeks to change our value perspective, to get us to affirm all life as having inherent worth, so that it becomes natural to speak of misfortune and harm occurring to all kinds of living organisms. The virtue of compassion is then expanded to imply dispositions to feel compassion in response to misfortunes, on appropriate occasions and in appropriate ways, and where possible to alleviate or prevent misfortunes. Again, ethical mysticism provides experiences that make us feel at home in the universe. In and through actively caring for specific lives, we experience unity with all life.

There is a danger that expanding compassion and suffering to all life will weaken the moral significance of pain. Schweitzer is well aware, however, that sentient creatures place special moral demands on us. In general, he devotes far more attention to sentient creatures than to plants and non-conscious animals. For example, as a physician he understands the need to test new drugs on animals, but he also insists on doing everything possible to mitigate the animals' pain. And he pleads for all of us to stop shutting our eyes to the brutality inflicted on animals used for food.[36] He does not make similar statements about experimentation on plants and non-sentient animals.

Moreover, sentient animals make special claims on us and limit the extent of human rights to liberty. In particular, it is more compassionate to kill mercifully than to permit a slow and painful death of domestic animals we can no longer take care of.[37] Again, a compassionate person condemns killing for mere amusement, as in bullfighting and hunting for sport, but he acknowledges the need to kill for food and self-defence.[38] In general, the responsibilities not to kill and not to harm animals are subordinate to compassion.[39]

Suffering humanity is always foremost in Schweitzer's thought. In an early sermon, delivered when he was 25 years old, he focused on the theological problem of evil: How can God allow so much horrible suffering? Although the sermon uses the language of conventional religion, it transcends mere homily and enunciates themes that are developed in his later thought. Traditional religion interprets much suffering as imposed by God, whether as a trial, a punishment or a condition for human freedom. In doing so, unfortunately, it imposes additional suffering on individuals who experience God as a judge rather than a merciful parent. Given Schweitzer's agnosticism about supernatural beings, it is better to resign ourselves to ignorance of the ultimate meaning of suffering. Compassion, then, can be offered and accepted in the spirit of Jesus' remark: 'Blessed are those who suffer, for they shall be comforted.'[40] This means comforting (sentient) sufferers in a spirit of love, even though we cannot remove all suffering. Such 'creative suffering' deepens the meaning we find in life, perhaps by forcing us to appreciate what matters most, or perhaps by bringing us closer to family and friends.

Later Schweitzer is more emphatic that we must resign ourselves to the mystery of suffering. This resignation, however, transforms compassion into a spiritual virtue that connects us with other lives. Compassion unifies us because it targets elemental features of all life: fragility, vulnerability to misfortune, death. Typically, compassion interweaves altruism and self-concern. It would not be compassion without a core of altruism. At the same time, there is an element of truth in Hobbes's contention that compassion arises from the painful imagining that the misfortune that happens to another might also happen to us.[41] As one of the most intense moral emotions, compassion is a potent source of moral motivation towards complete strangers and towards animals.

Asian religions deepen our grasp of compassion as a spiritual virtue. The Jain principle of *ahimsa* – do not kill or harm living creatures – has momentous, if not culminating, importance in the spiritual history of humanity. In its original formulation, *ahimsa* was justified in terms of personal purification, not other-oriented compassion.[42] The motive and reason given for not killing is to keep ourselves undefiled, rather than concern for the life taken. As a result, Jainism turned inward and emphasized refraining from harm, thereby falling short of an active ethics of love and helping.

Compassion is even more central in Buddhism. The first of the Noble Truths of Buddhism tells us that life is suffering, and that implies that to value life is to respond with compassion. Like the Jains, the Buddha emphasized avoidance of harm with less attention to active helping, in a spirit of optimism about improving lives. Only later does active helping become paramount in Mahayana Buddhism.[43] In general, Schweitzer criticizes Indian philosophy for veering towards 'world and life negation', and asceticism and non-involvement in improving the world.[44] At the same time, he praises Indian philosophy for tending to widen the moral circle to include all life. In contrast, Jesus provides a fuller development of compassion as active helping in response to suffering. Reverence for life widens Jesus' love to all life, wedding Christian compassionate love to Jain and Buddhist themes of valuing all life.[45]

Schweitzer's discussion of Asian religions, it might be noted, confirms the suggestion made above about the scope of compassion and suffering. For Schweitzer, the objects of compassion, that is, the things to which it is an intelligible response, include more than physical pain and mental anguish. Suffering is expanded to include death itself, minor and major frustrations, and other misfortunes, as when he sympathetically cites the Buddha's first Noble Truth: '"Birth is suffering, old age is suffering, death is suffering, to be united with what one loves not is suffering, to be separated from what one loves is suffering, not to attain one's desires is suffering."'[46]

Finally, although Schweitzer over-generalizes about 'Indian thought', he deserves credit for building bridges between Christian and Asian religious traditions.[47] He also bridges secular and spiritual traditions by understanding the core of religion as ethics rather than worldviews and dogmas. The most important question to ask of any religious tradition, at least after inquiring whether it makes demonstrably false claims, is how effectively it motivates responsible moral conduct – 'how far it produces permanent and profound incentives to the inward perfecting of personality and to ethical activity'.[48] And compassion is a primary source of moral motivation, especially when its scope is broadened to include misfortunes in addition to suffering.

To conclude, the ideal and virtue of compassion is central to reverence for life. The fellowship of those who bear the mark of pain is an idea used to highlight human unity, whereas the community of suffering is a broader idea intended to affirm a similar unity of all life. Both ideas emphasize the fragility and vulnerability of life, but they transform those features into creative possibilities for caring. Gratitude has similar creative possibilities, as we see next.

## Notes

1 Albert Schweitzer, *Out of My Life and Thought: An Autobiography*, trans. Antje Bultmann Lemke (Baltimore, MD: Johns Hopkins Press, 1998), p. 242.
2 Ibid., p. 223.
3 Ibid., p. 73.
4 Ibid., p. 242.
5 Albert Schweitzer, *Goethe: Five Studies*, trans. Charles R. Joy (Boston, MA: Beacon Press, 1961), p. 18; Albert Schweitzer, *Indian Thought and Its Development*, trans. Mrs Charles E.B. Russell (Gloucester, MA: Peter Smith, 1977), p. 102.
6 Albert Schweitzer, *Memoirs of Childhood and Youth*, trans. Kurt Bergel and Alice R. Bergel (Syracuse, NY: Syracuse University Press, 1997), p. 39.

7 Ibid., pp. 37–40.
8 Edgar Berman, *In Africa with Schweitzer* (New York: Harper and Row, 1986), pp. 188–93.
9 Louise Jilek-Aall, *Working With Dr Schweitzer* (Blaine, WA: Hancock House, 1990), pp. 137–9.
10 Albert Schweitzer, *The Psychiatric Study of Jesus: Exposition and Criticism*, trans. Charles R. Joy (Gloucester, MA: Peter Smith, 1975).
11 Albert Schweitzer, *The Primeval Forest*, trans. C.T. Campion (New York: Pyramid Books, 1961), p. 42.
12 Berman, *In Africa with Schweitzer*, pp. 62–6.
13 On Schweitzer's effectiveness as a physician see James Brabazon, *Albert Schweitzer: A Biography*, 2nd edn (Syracuse, NY: Syracuse University Press, 2000), p. 248; and John A.M. Karefa-Smart, 'Albert Schweitzer, Physician', in David C. Miller and James Pouilliard (eds), *The Relevance of Albert Schweitzer at the Dawn of the 21st Century* (Lanham, MD: University Press of America, 1992), pp. 57–61.
14 Schweitzer, *The Primeval Forest*, p. 128.
15 Schweitzer, *Memoirs of Childhood and Youth*, p. 73.
16 Brabazon, *Albert Schweitzer*, p. 301.
17 Arthur W. Frank, *The Wounded Storyteller* (Chicago, IL: University of Chicago Press, 1995), pp. 35–7, 49–50, 91–2, 118.
18 Albert Schweitzer, *Philosophy of Civilization*, trans. C.T. Campion (Amherst, NY: Prometheus Books, 1987), pp. 107, 305.
19 Albert Schweitzer, *A Place for Revelation: Sermons on Reverence for Life*, trans. David Larrimore Holland (New York: Irvington, 1993), p. 16.
20 Cf. Shelley E. Taylor, *The Tending Instinct* (New York: Henry Holt and Company, 2002).
21 Schweitzer, *A Place for Revelation*, p. 18.
22 Schweitzer, *Philosophy of Civilization*, p. 318.
23 Schweitzer, *A Place for Revelation*, p. 42.
24 Schweitzer, *Memoirs of Childhood and Youth*, p. 85.
25 Schweitzer, *A Place for Revelation*, pp. 94–110.
26 Ibid., p. 104.
27 Ibid., p. 20.
28 Ibid.
29 Ibid., p. 30.
30 Edmund D. Pellegrino and David C. Thomasma take note of the importance of professional distance, but they overstate the role of co-suffering in *The Virtues in Medical Practice* (New York: Oxford University Press, 1993), pp. 79–81.
31 Schweitzer, *Out of My Life and Thought*, p. 242.
32 Schweitzer, *A Place for Revelation*, p. 40; Schweitzer, *Philosophy of Civilization*, p. 316.
33 Schweitzer, *Philosophy of Civilization*, p. 255.
34 Schweitzer, *Out of My Life and Thought*, p. 242.
35 Albert Schweitzer, 'The Problem of Ethics in the Evolution of Human Thought', in Friends of Albert Schweitzer (eds), *To Dr Albert Schweitzer: A Festschrift Commemorating His 80th Birthday* (New York: Profile Press, 1955), p. 137. Cf. Schweitzer, *A Place for Revelation*, p. 11; and Albert Schweitzer, *The Teaching of Reverence for Life*, trans. Richard and Clara Winston (New York: Holt, Rinehart and Winston, 1965), p. 26.
36 Schweitzer, *Philosophy of Civilization*, pp. 318–19.
37 Schweitzer, *Indian Thought and Its Development*, p. 83.
38 Schweitzer, *A Place for Revelation*, pp. 28–9.
39 Schweitzer, *Indian Thought and Its Development*, p. 84.

40 Schweitzer, *Reverence for Life*, p. 17.

41 Thomas Hobbes, 'On Human Nature', in *The English Works of Thomas Hobbes* (London, 1845) Vol IV, ch. 9. Discussed by James Rachels, *The Elements of Moral Philosophy*, 4th edn (New York: McGraw-Hill, 2003), pp. 66–7.

42 Schweitzer, *Indian Thought and Its Development*, p. 80.

43 Ibid., pp. 103, 123.

44 Ibid., pp. 1–2.

45 Schweitzer, *Out of My Life and Thought*, p. 235.

46 The Buddha, quoted in Schweitzer, *Indian Thought and Its Development*, p. 96.

47 In particular, see Ara Paul Barsam, 'Albert Schweitzer, Jainism, and Reverence for Life', in Marvin Meyer and Kurt Bergel (eds), *Reverence for Life: The Ethics of Albert Schweitzer for the Twenty-First Century* (Syracuse, NY: Syracuse University Press, 2002), pp. 207–45.

48 Albert Schweitzer, *Christianity and the Religions of the World*, trans. Johanna Powers (New York: George H. Doran, 1923), pp. 40–41.

# Chapter 7

# Gratitude: Good Fortune Obligates

> I must not accept this good fortune as a matter of course, but must give something in return.[1]

Good fortune, good luck, the favourable accidents of birth and circumstance – are these things ours to enjoy without moral strings attached? Or should we recognize a *good fortune principle*: We are obligated to help others in return for our good fortune? If so, help whom, in what ways, and how much? Schweitzer argues that our good fortune is significantly shaped by the cumulative good will of others, in ways that generate responsibilities of gratitude. Meeting these responsibilities sustains moral community and draws us into wider spiritual relationships.

Herbert Spiegelberg, Schweitzer's fellow Alsatian, contends that the good fortune principle is justified by an egalitarian theory of justice. This chapter begins by rejecting his interpretation and several others, before establishing gratitude as its justification. It goes on to explore Schweitzer's conception of gratitude as a cardinal virtue, showing its relevance to contemporary discussions. The chapter concludes by noting that gratitude needs to be balanced by justice – ironically, the value to which Spiegelberg mistakenly traces the good fortune principle.

## Justifying the Good Fortune Principle

As a college student, Schweitzer found it inconceivable that he could pursue a relatively privileged life without contributing to the well-being of others. He felt he 'must give something in return' for his good fortune.[2] In this and most contexts, 'good fortune' means being well off compared to disadvantaged individuals.[3] The 'must' indicates that giving is a moral requirement rather than an optional good.

This felt obligation was clearly a major motive in Schweitzer's life and thought, but the justification of the good fortune principle is less obvious. Spiegelberg claims it lies in 'Schweitzer's ethical egalitarianism', a conception of justice aimed at equal distribution of basic resources.[4] It is unfair for some people to enjoy great luxury when others are severely disadvantaged. It is unjust in terms of 'cosmic justice' that requires us to nullify the 'unjust enrichment' created through accidents of birth and circumstance. Acting on the good fortune principle helps restore justice through individual initiatives to promote equality. Spiegelberg draws parallels with John Rawls's theory of justice as fairness, which seeks to counterbalance accidents of natural advantage and disadvantage; indeed, Spiegelberg's earlier writings influenced Rawls.[5] Although Schweitzer's views of justice do have some striking parallels with those of Rawls, as discussed in Chapter 8, Spiegelberg appears to misread Schweitzer through the distorting lens of his own egalitarian ethics.

There is no compelling evidence that justice is the foundation of the good fortune principle, much less for ascribing to Schweitzer an egalitarian theory of justice. Remarkably, Spiegelberg's only evidence is Schweitzer's refusal as a child to wear clothing of the gentry because it made him stand out from less-privileged children. That childhood event is hardly a convincing proof, if only because the context suggests a motive of peer-acceptance as much as justice.[6] Moreover, Schweitzer calls for individuals who enjoy especially good fortune to 'show more than average devotion' to others, not to redistribute their wealth in accord with an egalitarian standard.[7] He emphatically rejects communism.

Schweitzer does highlight one role for justice in generating obligations to help, but he has in mind compensatory rather than distributive justice. Compensatory justice requires us to make reparations for our past and present wrongdoing, both as individuals and as members of groups. In particular, Westerners must atone for their collective guilt for atrocities against Africans in slave trading, massive thefts of land and exploitation of resources, and the spread of disease and alcoholism while withholding essential medical care.[8] Whereas distributive justice concerns the fair allocation of resources, compensatory justice more narrowly concerns guilt and making amends for causing harm. In contrast, the good fortune principle centres on well-being, something for which we are not culpable. Schweitzer highlights the difference in the concluding chapter of *On the Edge of the Primeval Forest*. There he devotes several pages to showing that compensatory justice requires reparations for harm to Africans.[9] Juxtaposed in a separate section, he sets forth the good fortune principle, as it applies to suffering. Individuals who are helped to escape great suffering should do their part in providing humanitarian aid. This fellowship of those who bear the mark of pain is a fellowship of compassionate and reciprocal helping, not guilt for causing harm.

Is compassion, then, the basis for the good fortune principle? No, for compassion is a caring response to suffering and additional misfortunes, whereas the good fortune principle is focused on personal privilege and invites a wider range of helping. Schweitzer often links compassion and the good fortune principle without deriving one from the other. In particular, he distinguishes two 'great experiences' in his childhood that 'slowly became interwoven' to shape his life and thought: (1) compassion – 'being deeply stirred by the suffering in the world around us', and (2) 'wrestling with the problem of whether we have a right to good fortune'.[10] There he also alludes to the fellowship of those who bear the mark of pain, calling on individuals who have suffered and been helped to alleviate the suffering of others. As the wellspring of his humanitarian service, then, compassion and the good fortune principle are interwoven but have distinct moral values.

Does religion ground the good fortune principle? Once again there is a link: 'Unto whomsoever much is given, of him much shall be required' (Luke 12:48).[11] This scripture, however, rephrases rather than justifies the good fortune principle. In general, Schweitzer does not appeal to the authority of the scripture or divine commandments. Instead, he seeks a foundation for moral and religious claims in Reason – that is, within comprehensive and sound moral reasoning.

Finally, is the good fortune principle justified by the ideal of reverence for life? It is more accurate to say the principle is a key component of reverence for life as a unifying ideal. Moreover, when he conjoins the good fortune principle and reverence for life, the context is responsibility to persons, not to all animals and plants: 'Whatever more than others you have received in health, natural gifts, working capacity, success, a beautiful childhood, harmonious family circumstances, you must not accept as being a matter of course. You must pay a price for them. You must show more than average devotion of life to life.'[12] Rather than deriving the good fortune principle from the ideal of valuing all life, he merely bridges them with a metaphor: 'Just as the wave cannot exist for itself, but is ever a part of the heaving surface of the ocean, so must I never live my life for itself, but always in the experience which is going on around me.'[13] This is one of the many striking metaphors expressing his ethical mysticism, his sense that all life is ultimately one. In this way, ethical mysticism underlies both the good fortune principle and the ideal of valuing all life.

The justification of the good fortune principle is not justice, compassion, divine commands or reverence for all life. It is gratitude. In his popular addresses, Schweitzer makes this connection explicit: 'Whatever you have received more than others – in health, in talents, in ability, in success, in a pleasant childhood, in harmonious conditions of home life – all this you must not take to yourself as a matter of course. In gratitude for your good fortune, you must render in return some sacrifice of your own life for other life.'[14] The same justification is indicated, almost in passing, in discussing the fellowship of those who bear the mark of pain. Commenting on people freed from great pain, he writes that 'their gratitude should be the source of the gifts needed' to fund and implement international efforts to relieve suffering.[15] Gratitude is even alluded to in a radio address cited by Spiegelberg, who somehow fails to discern it: 'we must not accept what comes to us in our life by way of good luck as a matter of course, but have to make a sacrifice of thanksgiving for it by some act of help or service.'[16]

Additional evidence for gratitude as the foundation of the good fortune principle will be presented as we proceed. But let us turn at once to Schweitzer's conception of gratitude as it pertains to the reciprocal generosity enjoined by the good fortune principle.

## Importance of Gratitude

Most of us think of gratitude as a relatively minor virtue, at least compared to justice, compassion and honesty. Schweitzer dramatically elevates its importance and makes it central to his ethical outlook, along with authenticity and compassion. Gratitude is a cardinal virtue and more: it is 'a mysterious law of existence', in obedience to which we 'fulfill our destiny'.[17] It is a fundamental ideal that, like compassion, orients self-realization in service to others. It is mysterious in that to live by gratitude is to experience spiritual unity through ties of reciprocal giving and receiving.

Schweitzer uses many metaphors to convey this unity. In addition to the image of ocean waves and the fellowship of suffering, he says we are like wild plants that seem independent but which have common roots merged beneath the soil.[18] In this case, the roots are relationships of reciprocal giving and receiving. Gratitude enables us to appreciate the sources of our good fortune while supporting other persons' moral commitments by making them feel appreciated for their efforts. Ingratitude, by contrast, damages moral community by making people feel unappreciated and hence less likely to help others.[19]

In a similar vein, closer to our own time, Paul Camenisch invites us to understand gratitude as 'an entire outlook on life' and as 'the dominant mood or theme of a total way of life': 'The person or group living out of such a comprehensive sense of gratitude will live with a joyful sense of the interrelatedness of things whereby life is enriched by the generosity of persons or powers outside themselves. … [T]hey will see much of life's goodness grounded outside themselves in the uncoerced, undeserved bounty of other agencies well-disposed toward them.'[20]

Just so, Schweitzer would say. If there is a difference in the two thinkers, it is that Schweitzer emphasizes responsibilities whereas Camenisch downplays obligations (to be grateful) and guilt (for ingratitude). He believes that emotions of gratitude are not sufficiently subject to our direct control to be obligatory, although perhaps he underestimates the extent to which we can indirectly shape our emotions by shaping our attitudes.[21] At the same time, Camenisch recognizes there are obligations to act in appropriate ways in showing appreciation for gifts. The good fortune principle can be viewed as saying that obligatory appreciation for gifts includes giving back to others. In tune with both Schweitzer and Camenisch, when speaking of owing gratitude, I have in mind responsibilities of reciprocal giving motivated at least in part by good will, rather than obligations to have emotions.

## Whom we Owe, Whom to Help

Usually we think of gratitude as the appropriate response to parents, spouses, friends and other individuals who directly help us because they care about us. Schweitzer dramatically expands the circle of individuals to whom we owe gratitude. Indeed, the good fortune principle seems to apply to all good fortune (at least relative to disadvantaged persons), whatever its source. Occasionally he even speaks of a debt of gratitude owed to animals used in experiments that benefit us, and to nature itself.[22] Here it seems more plausible to speak of gratitude *for* benefits, rather than *to* animals and nature. Indeed, in his more careful moments, he writes of 'solidarity' with the animals used in experiments.[23] He is aware that in paradigm cases gratitude is owed in part because of motives of good will.

As Fred Berger notes, in paradigm instances gratitude 'does not consist in the requital of benefits but in a response to *benevolence*; it is a response to a grant of benefits (or the attempt to benefit us) which was motivated by a desire to help us.'[24] The good fortune principle is compatible with what Berger says. Indeed, Schweitzer frequently reminds us that gratitude is owed because of the kind or friendly intention, the 'will for good directed in your favor'.[25] Certainly he devotes most attention to good fortune created by people who help us from motives and intentions of caring, rather than entirely self-interested motives.

The circle of persons to whom we owe gratitude expands as we reflect on the extent to which we have benefited from others' beneficence. Ultimately, all benefits in our lives are in some way derived from the good will of others: 'Nothing [good] that may happen to you is purely accidental. Everything can be traced back to a will for good directed in your favor.'[26] Again, we all live by 'what others gave us in significant moments in our lives'; we should 'think in gratitude of those who have kindled flames within'.[27]

Consider a few examples. In a 1918 sermon containing an early statement of the good fortune principle, Schweitzer tells his congregation that gratitude is owed by survivors of the First World War to soldiers who died on their behalf.[28] In a later sermon he says we owe gratitude to teachers who enable us to develop our interests, talents, commitments and intelligence.[29] We also owe gratitude to health professionals who help restore our health. More fully, the patient recovering from an operation appropriately feels gratitude towards her physicians, nurses and other hospital staff, but also towards the scientists who made the discoveries that rendered the surgery possible. In addition, gratitude is owed to the philanthropists who establish and support the hospital with their donations, and to volunteers in the clinical tests of drugs used in the operation.

Are not soldiers, physicians, nurses, teachers and other professionals merely doing their job? This 'merely' is the commonest excuse used to avoid gratitude.[30] To say, for example, that no gratitude is owed to teachers because they are merely performing their duties is to devalue them by eclipsing their motives of caring for students. This reduction of motives to self-seeking is all too common today. In fact, it is the dominant (though not exclusive) ideology in academic disciplines such as economics, psychology, political science and sociobiology. Schweitzer's view of gratitude challenges all these reductive ideologies.[31]

Even when altruism is present, it might be objected that soldiers, philanthropists, volunteers and many professionals who contribute to our good fortune had no intention to benefit us in particular. Most of them did not even know us. Schweitzer does not consider this objection, but we can offer a reply on his behalf.[32] Some intentions of good will to others are open-ended or indefinite, rather than focused on particular individuals. They take the form, 'I want to help others' or 'I want to help other people who are in need of the service I can offer.' Insofar as our good fortune falls under the scope of these intentions, gratitude is the appropriate response for benefits received. And insofar as we receive more than average benefits, we have responsibilities to give more than average gifts in return.

We should distinguish, however, between the individuals to whom we owe gratitude and persons to whom we give in expressing gratitude. It is impossible to express gratitude directly to all our benefactors.[33] Perhaps their influence on us is unknown and not easily discoverable. Perhaps they are dead, as with soldiers and the many philanthropists who contributed to the social practices and institutions that enrich our lives. Or perhaps they do not need our reciprocal services, beyond a simple thank you. How, then, can we owe them anything, at least by way of active giving rather than simply feeling grateful? It might seem that debts of gratitude are limited by opportunities to reciprocate to specific benefactors. As Terrance McConnell suggests, 'if one has developed the disposition to provide a benefactor with a benefit on a suitable occasion and responsive to a real need [of the benefactor], one has done all that gratitude demands at that point. If the suitable occasion never arises, gratitude demands no more.'[34]

Disagreeing with McConnell, Schweitzer says we should express our gratitude indirectly, in the form of serial reciprocity. We should give to individuals who need our help, acting in the spirit of the 'inaccessible benefactors' who helped us.[35] Thus, our debt to dead soldiers is paid in part by ensuring that the soldiers' families are properly cared for, and in part by committing ourselves to creating a more humane society. Future-oriented service affirms solidarity with the past, in the same way that we honour and keep faith with a dead relative or friend by making a sacrifice on their behalf.

There is a danger, of course, that expanding the circle of gratitude could deflect attention from those to whom we owe most; it could also diffuse helping by spreading our efforts thin. The multiplication of those to whom we owe gratitude might also lead a few individuals to devote too much of their time and resources in service, at the expense of other important responsibilities. As we have seen, Schweitzer has been criticized for sacrificing his family by placing his mission in Africa above daily contact with his wife and daughter. Yet surely Schweitzer can recognize degrees of primacy among the debts of gratitude, and he is well aware of the need to set priorities among responsibilities. He also recognizes that gratitude is a virtue of reciprocal generosity, not an endless sum of debts to be paid. Like all virtues, gratitude must be balanced with other important virtues and responsibilities.

## How to Help and How Much

How much does the good fortune principle require of us? Initially Schweitzer entertained the possibility of formulating rough rules of thumb about how much to give.[36] Thus he suggested simplifying one's lifestyle, forgoing luxuries in order to have resources to help others. Having done that, we should divide our remaining resources equally between disadvantaged individuals and ourselves. In carefully presenting his view only a few years later, however, Schweitzer abandoned the search for even general rules of thumb about giving.[37] How we use our property is a free decision, *if* we are motivated by gratitude and other moral ideals in reverence for life.[38] The danger, of course, is that our predominant self-seeking will eclipse service, and that danger needs to be constantly borne in mind. Nevertheless, in his view, an ethics of virtues and ideals, of gratitude and genuineness, provides all the guidance we need or can have.

Rather than stating a precise rule of conduct, the good fortune principle expresses the ideal and virtue of gratitude. It also expresses related ideals of keeping faith with individuals whose good will contributes to our lives, honouring their beneficence through serial, reciprocal caring for others. As an ethics of ideals and virtues, with a markedly individualistic cast, reverence for life renounces any hierarchy of rules for balancing philanthropic responsibilities against responsibilities to family, friends, work and oneself. As we have seen, in opposing the usual emphasis on moral rules, Schweitzer states that decisions about how much is owed are subjective and arbitrary, but such statements are misleading.[39] Like all important decisions,

decisions about giving require good judgment in exercising virtues and balancing the conflicting demands of competing ideals. They are subjective only in that they allow considerable room for discretion and they are linked to personal projects of love.

Even assessing good fortune has a discretionary dimension. Not only is the relevant comparison group unclear, but good fortune itself has a personal aspect, namely, how we experience the objective benefits available to us.[40] Some individuals are miserable with their wealth, while others find joy in relatively modest benefits. Hence the sheer capacity for happiness and enjoyment of our fortune is one dimension of good fortune. At the same time, Schweitzer takes for granted that good fortune is primarily an objective matter that *ought* to be recognized and appreciated. Each of us is responsible for learning to feel appropriate gratitude for benefits, and we should refrain from criticizing others for their perceptions of what is required for them.[41]

How do we go about meeting our good fortune responsibilities? Some individuals do so by 'going beyond' minimum decency in pursuing their work, whether in service-oriented professions or in business.[42] Most of us, however, do so through philanthropy – through voluntary giving for public purposes, whether the gifts are money or time, local or international in scope, and whether the purposes are religious, humanitarian, cultural, political or environmental.[43] This giving in response to our good fortune is obligatory but also voluntary, in the sense of non-coerced.

Philanthropic responsibilities call for personal expression, for discovering our own way to help through personal projects of love, according to our opportunities, interests and talents.[44] Service is most strongly evoked in a personal calling, an idea that can be understood in religious or humanistic terms as projects of caring. A calling might be relatively focused in philanthropy, or it might be embedded in professions, family and other activities.[45] We should be cautious about the spectacular gesture, instead seeking more modest acts of helping in response to specific needs.[46] At the same time, there is a need for 'spiritual adventurers' whose service arises in a natural way, as a matter of felt duty, rather than from restless aspirations.[47]

Schweitzer urges us to find our own ways to serve, rather than emulating him directly: 'You can have your Lambaréné anywhere.'[48] Personal expression is important in order for service to contribute to self-realization, as well as for additional reasons which he leaves implicit. One such reason is that much of the value in helping is found in the caring expressed, and in the caring relationship established, rather than simply the good consequences of gifts. Caring implies personal identification with the causes and individuals we support, and that identification emerges from within rather than being imposed from without.[49] Just as our good fortune is a product of the good will of others, so we should help in expressing good will. Another reason why helping must be personal is in order to benefit recipients most effectively. The general good is promoted when individuals take personal initiative in responding to others' needs.[50] Still another reason for personal discretion is that helping should be ongoing, rather than rare, and we continue to help over long periods of time only when doing so brings satisfaction. Indeed, part of our good fortune resides in finding satisfaction in helping others.[51]

Schweitzer's individualism, it should be added, affects his attitudes towards philanthropic organizations. He is well aware that organizations are important in dealing with the magnitude of contemporary social problems, but he cautions that they easily become impersonal. Organizations need the '*personal initiative*, the diversely flexible power of the individual' who volunteers time and work.[52] At the same time, his decision to serve in Africa was in part shaped by his desire for 'absolutely personal and independent activity' that was not circumscribed by the demands of organizations.[53] Of course a hospital is an organization, and Schweitzer is not especially diplomatic in sharing authority within his hospital, nor wise in preparing for the transition of its administration after his death.[54]

## Gratitude and Justice

Schweitzer is sensitive to how power imbalances can distort moral values, but not sensitive enough. In this connection he notes that demands for gratitude are frequently inappropriate: 'All of us are strongly tempted to use the good we do as a trap to ensnare another', and we have 'misused gratitude to blackmail' and to humiliate.[55] Anger at the ingratitude of people we help is most often a form of self-righteousness that manifests motives of power and domination. With these remarks in mind, it is disconcerting to hear him occasionally complain about the ingratitude of the Africans he helped.

For example, he reports annoyance when a chief failed to show gratitude by failing to get his relatives to provide some labour for the hospital in return for medical services in dressing a minor gun wound: 'I have to threaten to stop dressing his hand and let it "go bad," and as no danger is involved I do, in fact, carry out my threat by not looking at his hand for three or four days.'[56] This insistence that his beneficiaries show gratitude goes beyond his quite reasonable policy of requiring some payment for the services he provided, for those who could afford to do so, even though the payment was far below the actual cost of providing the services. It is one thing for these modest payments to be required as part of accepting responsibility within a professional–client relationship. It is quite another thing when the payments become part of teaching patients to feel and express gratitude within the framework of a colonialist mission. Schweitzer speaks of the payment for services as a 'present made in return', and he complains that those who failed to feel gratitude for what he did was a sign that they had 'sunk even below the level of savages'.[57]

Taken in context, within the life of an extraordinarily caring physician and generous philanthropist, these complaints reveal Schweitzer as human, not inhumane. Few of us are willing to continue in a project of service, even on a very modest scale, in the absence of feeling appreciated for our efforts. Nevertheless, the complaints illustrate how relationships of gratitude are at risk within power imbalances, where they can lead to exploitation and domination.[58] If the danger is obvious in tyrannical parents, it is writ large in colonialism. Gratitude, like other virtues, needs to be integrated with a theory of justice.

A proverb enjoins, 'Be just before you are generous.' In a related vein, Charles Dickens parodies Mrs Jellyby for engaging in 'telescopic philanthropy' in viewing the needs of Africans from afar, while self-deceivingly being preoccupied with her own needs.[59] Schweitzer sometimes falls prey to the inverse danger of 'microscopic philanthropy': seeing needs and philanthropy from too close, so as to misperceive their wider social and political dimensions. If the ultimate goal in helping is to empower, then more attention needs to be paid to justice, which is our next topic.

## Notes

1 Albert Schweitzer, *Out of My Life and Thought*, trans. Antje Bultmann Lemke (Baltimore, MD: Johns Hopkins University Press, 1998), p. 82.
2 Ibid., p. 82.
3 For example, Albert Schweitzer, *The Teaching of Reverence for Life*, trans. Richard and Clara Winston (New York: Holt, Rinehart and Winston, 1965), p. 40.
4 Herbert Spiegelberg, 'Good Fortune Obligates: Albert Schweitzer's Second Ethical Principle', *Ethics*, 85 (1975): 227–34.
5 Spiegelberg develops his egalitarian conception of justice in 'A Defense of Human Equality', reprinted in *Steppingstones Toward an Ethics for Fellow Existers* (Dordrecht: Martinus Nijhoff, 1986), pp. 131–53. John Rawls refers to this essay in *A Theory of Justice*, revised edn (Cambridge, MA: Harvard University Press, 1999), p. 86.
6 Albert Schweitzer, *Memoirs of Childhood and Youth*, trans. Kurt Bergel and Alice R. Bergel (Syracuse, NY: Syracuse University Press, 1997), p. 15.
7 Albert Schweitzer, *Philosophy of Civilization*, trans. C.T. Campion (Amherst, NY: Prometheus Books, 1987), p. 321.
8 Albert Schweitzer, *Reverence for Life: Sermons 1909–1919*, trans. Reginald H. Fuller (New York: Irvington, 1993), p. 55.
9 Albert Schweitzer, *The Primeval Forest*, trans. C.T. Campion (New York: Pyramid Books, 1961), pp. 127–30.
10 Schweitzer, *Memoirs of Childhood and Youth*, pp. 73–4.
11 Albert Schweitzer, *Letters 1905–1965*, trans. Joachim Neugroschel, ed. Hans Walter Bahr (New York: Macmillan, 1992), p. 64.
12 Schweitzer, *Philosophy of Civilization*, p. 321.
13 Ibid., p. 321.
14 Albert Schweitzer, 'Your Second Job', *Reader's Digest*, 55 (October 1949), pp. 3–4. The second job is philanthropy (voluntary service), which elsewhere he refers to as 'secondary work' (Schweitzer, *Philosophy of Civilization*, p. 322).
15 Schweitzer, *The Primeval Forest*, p. 129.
16 Spiegelberg, 'Good Fortune Obligates', p. 228. Spiegelberg cites Schweitzer's 'Aus meinem Leben: Ein Vortrag', *Schweitzer Monatshefte*, 50 (1970): 1–7.
17 Schweitzer, *Reverence for Life*, p. 141.
18 Ibid.
19 Ibid., p. 129.
20 Paul F. Camenisch, 'Gift and Gratitude in Ethics', *The Journal of Religious Ethics*, 9 (1981): 23. The wide importance of gratitude in human lives is also explored in Robert A. Emmons and Michael E. McCullough (eds), *The Psychology of Gratitude* (New York: Oxford University Press, 2004).
21 Camenisch, 'Gift and Gratitude in Ethics', p. 2.
22 Albert Schweitzer, *A Place for Revelation: Sermons on Reverence for Life*, trans. David Larrimore Holland (New York: Irvington, 1993), p. 34. On linking gratitude and appreciation for life itself, see Thomas E. Hill, Jr, 'Ideals of Human Excellence and Preserving Natural Environments', in Thomas E. Hill, Jr, *Autonomy and Self-Respect* (New York: Cambridge University Press, 1991), pp. 104–17.

23 Schweitzer, *The Philosophy of Civilization*, p. 318.
24 Fred R. Berger, 'Gratitude', *Ethics*, 85 (1974/75): 299.
25 Schweitzer, *Reverence for Life*, p. 132.
26 Ibid., p. 132.
27 Schweitzer, *Memoirs of Childhood and Youth*, pp. 81–2.
28 Schweitzer, *Reverence for Life*, pp. 105–6. The 1919 humanistic sermons on gratitude stand in marked contrast with his religious 1904 sermon on gratitude. In other earlier sermons Schweitzer also discusses gratitude as a response to God's grace. Schweitzer, *Reverence for Life*, pp. 36–42, 75, 85, 93.
29 Schweitzer, *Reverence for Life*, pp. 139–40.
30 Ibid., p. 132.
31 So do contemporary thinkers like Amartya Sen, *On Ethics and Economics* (Oxford: Blackwell, 1987); and Alfie Kohn, *The Brighter Side of Human Nature* (New York: Basic Books, 1990).
32 Related arguments concerning philanthropy are developed by Lawrence C. Becker, *Reciprocity* (New York: Routledge and Kegan Paul, 1986), pp. 230–31; and Terrance McConnell, *Gratitude* (Philadelphia, PA: Temple University Press, 1993), pp. 28–9. Robert Nozick's objections in *Anarchy, State, and Utopia* (New York: Basic Books, 1974) are countered by Richard J. Arneson in 'The Principle of Fairness and Free-Rider Problems', *Ethics*, 92 (1982): 617–33. See also Alan D. Schrift (ed.), *The Logic of the Gift: Toward an Ethic of Generosity* (New York: Routledge, 1997).
33 Schweitzer, *Reverence for Life*, p. 139.
34 Terrence McConnell, *Gratitude*, p. 8.
35 Schweitzer, *Reverence for Life*, pp. 140–41.
36 Schweitzer, *A Place for Revelation*, pp. 62–3, 75–7.
37 Schweitzer, *Philosophy of Civilization*, p. 291.
38 Ibid., pp. 320–23.
39 Ibid., p. 320; Schweitzer, *Out of My Life and Thought*, p. 236.
40 Spiegelberg raises this question, although not in connection with gratitude. 'Good Fortune Obligates', p. 230.
41 Schweitzer, *Reverence for Life*, pp. 131–4.
42 Schweitzer, *Philosophy of Civilization*, p. 320.
43 This definition comes from Robert Payton, 'American Values and Private Philanthropy', in Kenneth W. Thompson (ed.), *Philanthropy: Private Means, Public Ends* (Lanham, MD: University Press of America, 1987), pp. 3–20; and Mike W. Martin, *Virtuous Giving: Philanthropy, Voluntary Service, and Caring* (Bloomington, IN: Indiana University Press, 1984), p. 1.
44 Schweitzer, *Philosophy of Civilization*, p. 322.
45 Ibid., pp. 305, 322.
46 Schweitzer, *A Place for Revelation*, p. 42; Schweitzer, *Out of My Life and Thought*, p. 88.
47 Schweitzer, *A Place for Revelation*, p. 85; Schweitzer, *Out of My Life and Thought*, p. 88.
48 Quoted by James Brabazon, *Albert Schweitzer: A Biography*, 2nd edn (Syracuse, NY: Syracuse University Press, 2000), p. 500. Cf. Schweitzer, *Out of My Life and Thought*, p. 88.
49 Cf. John O'Connor, 'Philanthropy and Selfishness', in Ellen Frankel Paul, Fred. D. Miller, Jr, Jeffrey Paul, and John Ahrens (eds), *Beneficence, Philanthropy and the Public Good* (Oxford: Blackwell, 1987), pp. 113–27.
50 Schweitzer, *Philosophy of Civilization*, p. 320.

51 Schweitzer, *Out of My Life and Thought*, p. 244. Cf. Anne Colby and William Damon, *Some Do Care: Contemporary Lives of Moral Commitment* (New York: Free Press, 1992), pp. 162, 261, 278–80.
52 Schweitzer, *A Place for Revelation*, p. 83.
53 Schweitzer, *Out of My Life and Thought*, pp. 82–5.
54 Edgar Berman, *In Africa with Schweitzer* (New York: Harper and Row, 1986).
55 Schweitzer, *Reverence for Life*, p. 128.
56 Schweitzer, *The Primeval Forest*, pp. 147–8.
57 Ibid., pp. 174, 227.
58 Cf. Claudia Card, 'Gratitude and Obligation', *American Philosophical Quarterly*, 25 (1988): 115–27.
59 Charles Dickens, *Bleak House* (New York: Bantam, 1983), pp. 32–43.

# Chapter 8

# Justice as Human Rights

> We call once more for justice ... filled to the full with the value of each single human existence.[1]

In celebrating Jesus' 'ethic of pure love', Schweitzer claims that social justice was unimportant to Jesus because he believed the world was about to end.[2] According to Henry Clark, this claim shows that 'Schweitzer explicitly rejects justice as an ideal for social ethics.'[3] Nothing could be further from the truth. Schweitzer insists that we, unlike Jesus, must have a theory of justice to protect individual liberty and advance civilization.[4] Schweitzer understands justice primarily in terms of human rights 'which guarantee to each person the greatest possible freedom for his personality within the entity of his own nation'.[5]

Schweitzer discusses four aspects of justice: respect for individual liberty (tolerance), fair distribution of economic benefits and burdens (economic justice), punishment (punitive justice) and compensation for harm (compensatory justice). His discussions are fragmentary, but they suggest directions he might have taken in completing the planned additional volumes of *The Philosophy of Civilization*. After exploring each aspect, this chapter responds to the objection that his participation in colonialism undermines reverence for life as an ethical theory.

## Liberty and Tolerance

Reverence for life affirms maximum individual freedom to interpret and apply moral ideals in the responsible pursuit of self-realization. Specifically, freedom of choice is needed in forming personal projects of love and in deciding how best to help others.[6] Protecting this freedom requires tolerance.

Tolerance is a slippery and ambiguous idea. Ija Pawlowska distinguishes three of its meanings: negative, positive and noncoercive tolerance. *Negative tolerance* means refraining (perhaps grudgingly) from criticizing beliefs and actions we consider morally wrong in order to maintain a pluralistic community, thereby withholding even the 'corrective influence' of criticism. *Positive tolerance* means celebrating the diversity of moral views and conduct, even when we disagree with them. *Noncoercive tolerance* means refraining from coercion, while permitting reasoned criticism of others' views.

Applying these distinctions, Pawlowska claims that Schweitzer 'was not tolerant in the sphere of morality either in the positive or in the negative sense of the word', given that he criticizes practices such as torture and oppression which violate reverence for life. Instead, he displays noncoercive tolerance in moral matters by making reasoned criticisms of views opposed to reverence for life, while shunning violence and coercion towards persons who hold those views.[7] Pawlowska also says Schweitzer is 'truly tolerant in the positive sense toward other religions', and she traces this acceptance to his indifference to religious dogmas.[8]

Pawlowska over-generalizes in several directions. For one thing, Schweitzer does not forbid all coercion and violence, although he portrays them as falling short of the ideal (as argued in Chapter 9). For another thing, when he disagrees with other views, he frequently manifests negative tolerance by withholding condemnation of persons and urging forgiveness.[9] For yet another thing, Schweitzer critiques religions for their mistaken moral beliefs and for their failure to respect reason (scholarship, science) and individual thought.

To expand on the last point, Schweitzer criticizes all religious groups, with the exception of the Quakers, for collaborating with harmful forms of nationalism and worldly power.[10] He also criticizes Asian religions for lacking sufficient moral optimism, even as he praises them for widening the circle of moral concern to include all life. And far from being indifferent to religious dogma, he rejects parochial dogmas in his quest for the historical Jesus. Because he regards religion largely as ethics, he sees far too much at stake to refrain from evaluating religious claims. His criticisms, however, are part of respectful interfaith dialogue. Inspired by how his father's church accommodated both Protestants and Catholics, he calls for worldwide religious reconciliation.[11] In short, Schweitzer's stance towards religion is complex: positive tolerance in celebrating spirituality and individualism, negative tolerance in refraining from self-righteous condemnations, noncoercive tolerance in critiquing but not coercing beliefs, and some limits on tolerance in all these senses.

What does tolerance imply concerning contemporary 'culture war' issues such as sexual practices, assisted suicide and abortion? Here we need to bear in mind the distinction between (a) the requirements of reverence for life, and (b) Schweitzer's personal interpretations and applications of those requirements. Reverence for life combines high ideals with wide latitude for responsible individualism in interpreting and implementing ideals. Hence we can embrace reverence for life while rejecting some of Schweitzer's personal applications of ideals, including the ideal of justice.

Regarding sexual practices, Schweitzer is conventional in his personal conduct but exceptionally open-minded (positively tolerant) about the conduct of others. As James Brabazon observes, he genuinely enjoys the 'kaleidoscope of character'.[12] Sexual indiscretions among the young doctors and nurses at Lambaréné are private matters, unless they disrupt hospital work.[13] When Schweitzer does make reasoned evaluations of sexual practices, his evaluations tend to be on the liberal side. For example, he accepts polygamy as one reasonable family arrangement in African societies that lack safety nets for women and children.[14] We do not know his views about sexual orientation, but his emphasis on authenticity in the pursuit of self-realization would seem to favour positive tolerance, within wide limits, of sexual conduct by consenting adults.

Regarding end-of-life issues, we know that Schweitzer opposes suicide, physician-assisted suicide and euthanasia. As was customary in his day, he believes that suicide is a symptom of mental imbalance, and hence incompatible with the mental health associated with reverence for self. He also believes that 'with a suffering person … I ought not shorten his life by even an hour.'[15] Schweitzer is also paternalistic towards his patients, as were most physicians in the decades preceding the 1960s patient-rights movement that made free and informed consent central to medicine. And in 1960, when medical technology had reached the point where it could sustain a human life in a vegetative state for many years, he tells Edgar Berman that he personally could not let a patient, especially a child, die by withholding medical care: 'it may be more merciful and even more ethical to let a [human] life expire … but I couldn't let life just expire.'[16]

Notice, however, that the tone of the last remark – 'but I couldn't' – implies a distinction between his personal views and what mercy requires of everyone. In general, Schweitzer's personal attitudes do not settle the requirements of reverence for life regarding end-of-life decisions. To be sure, reverence for life establishes a strong presumption against killing human beings, but the presumption is sometimes overridden by other moral considerations. Reverence for life makes a strong plea for compassion, which is a more comprehensive virtue than non-killing, and it acknowledges that death can come as deliverance from uncontrollable suffering at the end of life.[17] Moreover, he emphasizes that 'pain is a more terrible lord of mankind than even death.'[18] And at the end of his life Schweitzer reportedly refused life-extending therapies for himself.[19] Most important, reverence for life leaves wide latitude for individuals to reflect autonomously on these issues in the spirit of reverence for life. Self-realization extends to decisions about dying with dignity at the end of a long and fulfilling life, without being forced to accept futile, costly and degrading medical procedures.

Finally, consider abortion. Reverence for life contains a strong presumption against killing. If we focus exclusively on that presumption, then reverence for life seems to imply a conservative, pro-life stance that condemns abortion, except perhaps to save the life of the woman. One author even suggests that Schweitzer's refusal to rank life forms makes it irrelevant whether the developing foetus is a person; it is enough to observe that it is alive and has a will to live.[20] This is a misinterpretation. It matters enormously whether the life we are talking about is a person. Schweitzer values all life, but he emphasizes the special moral claims of persons. Only humans have human rights, and reverence for life does not tell us when a foetus becomes a human being with full rights.

Even after we form a judgment about when a person comes into existence, there are other important values to be considered, in particular women's rights to autonomy. Schweitzer was not a proto-feminist, and his personal attitudes towards women sometimes mirror the conventions of his day. Nevertheless, just as reverence for life establishes a strong presumption against killing, it provides strong support for the self-realization and autonomous decisions of all people – including women. It affirms the rights of all people to make decisions concerning their bodies, as well as decisions concerning their education, careers and personal projects of love. All things considered, reverence for life neither enjoins nor precludes a personal stance of pro-life or pro-choice on abortion, but it seems to favour social policies that respect freedom and tolerance about which stance to adopt in one's personal life.

Abortion dramatically illustrates why we must not seize on one aspect of Schweitzer's ethical theory and ignore other aspects, let alone adopt his personal applications of his theory as canonical for everyone. Reverence for life is a confluence of myriad moral ideals, unified and widened in their application so as to have spiritual dimensions, and those ideals include authenticity and self-realization as centrally as love and non-violence.

**Economic Justice**

Justice in distributing economic goods and services centres on property, which in 1919 struck Schweitzer as 'the most difficult and timely question of ethics'.[21] Schweitzer struggles with economic justice in three remarkable sermons when he first presents reverence for life.[22] In doing so, he seeks to balance and integrate self-realization with love.

On the one hand, both self-realization and the progress of civilization should lead us to celebrate individual initiative in pursuing wealth, given that wealth is vital to the survival and development of individuals, families and nations. Free exchange of property is equally essential. Accordingly, Schweitzer firmly rejects communism. At the same time, he understands that property is made possible by the laws and institutions that define and protect it. And much wealth is inherited, severing the tie between individual initiative and property. Ultimately, 'society is the master of property' and has the right to tax it for the general good.[23] Each country must work out its own balance of taxation and private ownership. Today these views seem sensible and commonplace, but Schweitzer speaks at a time when grand ideologies, including communism and fascism, distorted the common-sense of many intellectuals.

On the other hand, we have responsibilities rooted in justice, as well as in compassion and gratitude, to share our resources with people in desperate need of assistance. We should view ourselves as stewards over goods that we allocate between ourselves and others in a spirit of both compassion and self-realization.[24] Individuals should be given maximum liberty to exercise discretion about how they share and serve through projects of love. Essential service is provided by professionals, service workers and philanthropists. The same is true of business entrepreneurs who create jobs and wealth, although personal caring for their employees should temper harsh competitiveness.[25] Wealth should contribute to the general good, but it 'must reach the community in the most varied ways, if it is to be of the greatest benefit to all'.[26]

At this point, Schweitzer's discussion of social justice leaves off. It is tempting to speculate, however, about how reverence for life might be extended into contemporary debates about social and political justice, that is, justice in matters of basic institutions and practices. John Rawls provides the reference point for contemporary discussions of social justice, and it is illuminating to compare his views with Schweitzer's.

At first glance, their views seem wholly at odds, given that Rawls explicitly rejects ethical perfectionism. A closer look, however, shows that what Rawls means by perfectionism is not what Schweitzer has in mind. Rawls defines perfectionism as 'directing society to arrange institutions and to define the duties and obligations of individuals so as to maximize the achievement of human excellence in art, science, and culture'.[27] He distinguishes two versions of perfectionism. The strong, Nietzschean, version makes perfectionism the sole moral principle, thereby giving preference to an elite group of highly talented individuals. The moderate, Aristotelian, version regards perfectionism as one among several principles, which need to be balanced with each other. Rawls argues that even the moderate version should be rejected because it permits undemocratic favouritism towards talented individuals.

Like Rawls, Schweitzer rejects the strong, Nietzschean version. He might embrace the moderate version, but only if 'culture' is widened well beyond Rawls's sense. Rawls means excellence in the arts, sciences, humanities, education and historical preservation. Schweitzer's conception of civilization includes these things but it also includes many additional moral and spiritual ideals that advance civilization and define moral self-perfecting, for example compassion and respect for basic rights. Hence, Rawls does not explicitly engage Schweitzer's version of ethical idealism.

In place of perfectionism, Rawls defends his famous two principles of justice, as the basis for the view he calls 'justice as fairness':

> First [and paramount]: each person is to have an equal right to the most extensive scheme of equal basic liberties compatible with a similar scheme of liberties for other. Second: social and economic inequalities are to be arranged so that they are both (a) reasonably expected to be to everyone's advantage, and (b) attached to positions and offices open to all.[28]

Schweitzer is not enamoured of rules, much less of abstract theories such as the social contract theory Rawls uses to justify his principles. Moreover, whereas Schweitzer makes human rights fundamental in thinking about justice, Rawls derives rights from his two principles (duties) of justice, in effect making them societal or institutional rights (rights defined in terms of institutions), rather than rights defined in terms of being a human being. Nevertheless, reverence for life is very much in tune with the content of Rawls's two principles. The first principle enjoins maximum equal liberty, in particular respect for political rights possessed by each member of a society. This freedom is essential to the pursuit of self-realization, and connects with the affirmation of human rights. The second principle permits substantial differences in wealth and power, as long as the differences tend to promote the well-being of the most disadvantaged members of society. This concern for the disadvantaged, of course, is also a high priority in Schweitzer's ethic of love and compassion.

A remaining question is whether Schweitzer limits rights to basic liberties not to be interfered with, or whether he leaves room for welfare rights, that is, rights to receive survival goods from the community when one cannot earn them on one's own, and when the community has them available. Rawls believes in extensive welfare rights, although he expresses them in terms of duties to the disadvantaged rather than human rights. Now, the distinction between liberty and welfare rights had not been drawn clearly when Schweitzer wrote. His list of basic rights, however, includes at least one welfare right: the right to education. Beyond that, it is unclear how extensive his list of welfare rights would be. His emphasis on compassion seems to favour a safety net based on human rights to secure basic needs such as food, shelter and health care. At the same time, his strong moral individualism might favour allowing voluntary philanthropy to play the primary role in helping the disadvantaged, at least once minimum needs are met. Probably he would regard the extent of welfare rights, quite plausibly, as best left for political compromises within specific societies. In any case, here again reverence for life provides considerable latitude for applying moral ideals in alternative ways.

Finally, Schweitzer's discussion of property ends on a note relevant to the growing gap between rich and poor. We should live, he says, with an uneasy conscience – an uncomfortable awareness that we live in comfort while many others live in desperate poverty.[29] We must be willing to reflect, in honest and nuanced ways, on what is '*really* necessary' for our survival and flourishing, and on what compassion requires in alleviating desperate suffering.[30]

## Punishment and Compensation

Rights to life, liberty and property imply rights to self-defence. There are also duties to protect innocent life from harm and to support and protect valuable cultural institutions. These rights and duties must be secured through a system of justified punishment for serious violations of laws. Such punishment, of course, does not mean barbaric treatment of the sort found in many prisons today. And for minor crimes, punishment should involve compensation rather than prison.

The following episode at Lambaréné provides clues about the direction Schweitzer's views on punishment might have taken. He was awoken one morning by a loud dispute.[31] Without asking permission, a patient had used a man's boat to go fishing by moonlight. The boat's owner confronted him as he returned from fishing, demanding all the fish caught, along with additional monetary compensation, as required by local law. Because the boat was on hospital grounds, however, Schweitzer was asked to adjudicate the dispute. He ruled that each of the two men was partly in the right and partly in the wrong. The owner was owed compensation because his canoe was used without permission. He was at fault, however, for enticing wrongdoing by carelessly failing to padlock a chain securing his boat to a tree. In addition, he was guilty of laziness for failing to take advantage of the moonlight to go fishing himself. In turn, the patient was guilty of using the boat without permission, but he deserved recognition for his industriousness. As a penalty, Schweitzer ruled that one-third of the fish should go to the owner of the boat, one-third to the fisher for his labour, and one-third to the hospital because the offence took up the precious time of the hospital's chief administrator!

Taken out of context, the solution seems eccentric. Most of us regard the boat owner as imprudent but not culpable for failing to fasten the padlock, let alone for not going fishing himself. Moreover, we worry that allowing the thief to keep a third of the fish will encourage rather than deter future wrongdoing. Even so, Schweitzer had the authority to override local laws for offences committed on his property, and to use the occasion to encourage a new work ethic. Our interest here, however, is in Schweitzer's emphasis on restoring relationships and connecting punishment with a wider array of community values. This emphasis resonates with an emerging theory of punishment called restorative justice.

Restorative justice is an alternative to traditional retribution, utilitarianism and therapy. Retribution sees inherent worth in inflicting suffering in return for wrongdoing – if not an eye for an eye, at least some proportionate response. Utilitarianism appeals to the good consequences of punishment in deterring future crimes and in satisfying feelings of vengeance without vigilantes. Therapeutic approaches seek to rehabilitate criminals who are regarded as sick or immature. In contrast to these approaches, restorative theories emphasize reconciliation and restoration of broken relationships within communities. Restoration does not replace justice with mercy, but instead integrates them, for example by encouraging criminals to apologize to victims and fostering forgiveness of remorseful wrongdoers.[32]

As such, restorative justice captures much of the spirit of reverence for life. Schweitzer's resolution of the fishing dispute turns on fair compensation more than punishment – the midnight thief must provide compensation as part of making restitution. Stronger penalties are needed for violent crimes. But even when violence has occurred, especially collective violence during global conflicts, compensatory justice can be more effective than reciprocal cruelty. Thus Schweitzer calls for Western societies to pay debts of atonement and compensation for their cruelty towards and exploitation of African people.[33] Sometimes he cites atonement as his motive for going to Africa. And although justice is primarily a human-oriented concept, Schweitzer comments that one of our motives in helping animals should be to make amends for the harm done to other animals in medical experiments from which we all benefit.[34]

What about capital punishment? Most restorative-justice theorists oppose it, and so does Schweitzer: 'I am against the death penalty. We have no right to kill a human being. We have only the right to deprive him of his freedom if he constitutes a menace to human society.'[35] A critic might reply that capital punishment symbolically affirms the sacredness of life and the horror of killing innocent persons, even if capital punishment is not an effective deterrent. As for restorative justice, perhaps whatever reconciliation is possible could take place in the period between conviction and execution. The critic's suggestion might seem a stretch for anyone seriously committed to reverence for life, yet perhaps even here the emphasis on moral individualism in reverence for life leaves room for more than one reasonable view concerning capital punishment.

Of great importance, reverence for life affirms generous forgiving as an ideal.[36] It does so from two directions. One direction is in interpreting others' offences. Rather than seeing the worst in people, we should assume their acts of injustice are half owing to unfortunate circumstances, a quarter owing to ignorance, and only a quarter due to malevolence. The other direction is honesty with ourselves in applying the golden rule. Often we are guilty of comparable offences, and honesty forces us to forgive if we expect similar forgiveness from others. Even when we have an 'outward right' to be angry and resentful, we might not 'have the right inwardly'.[37] We should be willing to accept some injustice as atonement for our own wrongdoing. In this way, forgiving others should be motivated by honesty with ourselves, as well as by love.[38]

Even so, forgiveness is compatible with punishment. To forgive is to abandon anger, hate and blame for injustices committed against us and people we care about. But that does not mean accepting injury passively. Jesus tells us to forgive, to love our enemies and turn the other cheek. Yet we live in a world where passive acceptance of injustice fosters greater injustice. We have the right to defend ourselves and a duty to support innocent and oppressed people. Accordingly, we must balance the ideal of love with the ideals of justice and self-respect. Each of us must determine where to forgive and when to fight in defence of our lives and ideals.[39]

Finally, although reverence for life is flexible in integrating forgiveness with reasonable punishment, it is clear that in his personal life Schweitzer emphasizes forgiveness over punishment, and love over justice. A story about his childhood foreshadows this emphasis.[40] He and his friends mocked and taunted Mausche, a Jew who periodically visited the village on business. Once he joined his friends in throwing rocks at him.[41] He immediately felt the cruelty of the act and later befriended Mausche. We might expect the story to convey a nascent indignation (if not rage) against injustice, but instead Schweitzer reports being overwhelmed by Mausche's 'embarrassed, good-natured smile' and his silence in the face of persecution. Mausche becomes a symbol of patience and forgiveness. No doubt in a post-Holocaust world Mausche is a symbol we can no longer embrace. Yet the ideal of forgiveness, even as we hold individuals accountable for their wrongdoing, remains integral to the search for reconciliation, peace and restorative justice.

## Human Rights and Colonialism

For some observers, Schweitzer's mission of mercy becomes a tragic symbol of colonialist oppression. Does Schweitzer's participation in colonialism undermine his ethical theory? That would be like saying Thomas Jefferson's participation in slavery undermines his theory of human rights. Both thinkers had large moral blind spots in applying their ethical theories, but that is no basis for rejecting the theories in their entirety.

Schweitzer's views on colonialism are complex. On the one hand, he condemns its cruelties at a time when most of the Western world was overtly racist. He rejects colonialist practices as 'largely antagonistic' to civilized values.[42] Thus he speaks against the widespread practice of forced labour in Africa, insisting it is too high a price to pay for encouraging individuals to become responsible workers.[43] He opposes the direct imposition of Western customs, and he tolerates polygamy and other tribal traditions. He speaks passionately of Westerners' duties of atonement, compensation and restitution for the generations of harm done to the African people through slave trading, thefts of land, exploitation of resources, and the spread of disease and alcoholism.[44] Most important, he chooses to live most of his adult life among African people, deeply committed to alleviating their suffering, and inspiring many others to do so as well. Several times he characterizes his service at Lambaréné as part of the atonement whites owed to Africans for enslaving and exploiting them.[45]

On the other hand, Schweitzer is a paternalist who not only participates in colonialism but defends it as an interim system.[46] Although born of exploitation and cruelty, colonialism had become a necessary evil until African societies developed to the point where they could govern themselves in the modern world of international trade. Both tribalism and colonialism left Africans uneducated and undisciplined, in need of guidance from civilized societies. For Schweitzer at Lambaréné, the guidance included slapping hospital workers who failed to do their jobs. The forces of world trade led to their lost independence, and the only realistic and humane option at the time was paternalism: 'Have we whites the right to impose our rule on primitive and semiprimitive peoples? ... No, if we want only to rule and draw material advantage from their country. Yes, if we seriously desire to educate them and help them to attain a state of well-being.'[47] Although Africans deserve the respect and dignity owed to all persons, 'the negro is a child' towards whom Schweitzer would say 'I am your brother, it is true, but your elder brother.'[48]

Today these attitudes appal and enrage. To be sure, they need to be assessed in historical context. Among his peers, Schweitzer is progressive, even radical, in identifying and condemning the cruelties of colonialism and racism.[49] His cultural paternalism is an enormous advance over denying all kinship. Moreover, he is prescient about the widespread violence of tribal violence once colonialism is overthrown. Nevertheless, he has a seriously flawed moral understanding of colonialism.

W.E.B. DuBois offers a balanced assessment of Schweitzer as genuinely concerned for Africans as human beings, yet naïve about the missionary movement and lacking a 'broad grasp of what modern exploitation means, of what imperial colonialism has done to the world'.[50] Such a grasp would have led him to support a more rapid movement towards independent African nations, advanced education for Africans (rather than limiting them to manual work), and training Africans to take over his hospital at Lambaréné. DuBois goes too far, however, when he adds that if Schweitzer had such a grasp 'he probably would have tried to heal the souls of white Europe rather than the bodies of black Africa.' In criticizing Schweitzer's moral blind spots we should not downplay his extraordinary humanitarian service.

Does Schweitzer's collaboration with colonialism undermine his affirmation of human rights? His fullest statement about human rights is in the 1925 essay, 'The Relations of the White and Coloured Races', in which he calls for colonialist practices to be enlightened by respect for human rights. There he tells us that human rights 'can only be fully secured in a stable and well-ordered society'.[51] A dangerous, if not ominous, sentence follows: 'In a disordered society the very well-being of man himself often demands that his fundamental rights should be abridged.'[52] Africa became a continent of such societies, destroying the independence of Africans. As a consequence, respect for human rights is possible within a humane version of colonialism that gradually moves towards full recognition of these fundamental human rights: rights to habitation in areas where one is raised, freedom of movement, use and development of land, freedom to work and exchange goods and services, legal justice and protection, social organization, and education. Such rights need to be secured before moving to 'a new stable social organization' that will enable a full flourishing of human rights.[53]

The logic is seductive, but insidious. It takes historically-established colonialism as a given, then claims that human rights do not fully apply because of the loss of freedom under colonialism, and then enjoins making do with lesser rights until a gradual transition occurs from colonialism to a freer society. This reasoning would condemn all violent revolution, American or African, and postpone the restoration of rights indefinitely. Granted, the appeal to human rights has been abused as often as any other moral idea, causing unnecessary violence and war. But unless we are complete pacifists – and Schweitzer is not, as we will see in Chapter 9 – at times we must fight for liberty, even in some historical settings, by engaging in violent revolution. A sound human-rights ethics makes the exercise of rights central to well-being, not secondary to social prosperity.

Does reverence for life leave room for a passionate and sometimes life-sacrificing defence of liberty? In particular, was reverence for life relevant to Africans' fight for freedom from the tyranny of colonialism? In a letter written when he was 84, Schweitzer seems to deny its relevance: 'My idea of reverence for life is not meant to guide the African in striving for his own and his nation's freedom. It is meant to get him to deal with more than himself in the spiritual world, where he is occupied with his soul.'[54] Had Schweitzer come to believe that reverence for life applies only to character and not to social justice?

No. Most likely, the letter means that reverence for life does not provide a direct solution ('guide') to the struggle for African independence, but it is certainly relevant to that struggle. Consistent with his earlier views, he thought reverence for life provides a foundation for all dimensions of ethics, a foundation that allows maximum individual freedom of conscience in making personal decisions and establishing social policies and law. Schweitzer is convinced that social transformation must begin with spiritual change within individuals, as discussed in Chapter 9, but he is equally clear that reverence for life entails respect for rights. Hence, spiritual change of Africans, as for each of us, must emerge from an inner change of character as manifested in love, compassion and a sense of justice.

To conclude, reverence for life embodies a conception of human rights that affirms the dignity and worth of all persons, as shown in tolerance and respect for liberty, balanced affirmation of economic freedom and active concern for the disadvantaged, humane forms of punishment and compensation, and opposition to oppression. Properly applied, reverence for life condemns colonialism, slavery, genocide and other forms of social tyranny. Does maximum personal freedom require us to go further by construing reverence for life as only one contribution to justice, especially given its incompleteness? I believe it does. As Stuart Hampshire observes, there will never be complete agreement about justice because there will never be complete agreement about the good: 'Justice and fairness in substantial matters, as in the distribution of goods or in the payment of penalties for a crime, will always vary with varying moral outlooks and with varying conceptions of the good.'[55] Rather than trying to reach agreement on a detailed theory of cosmic fairness, we should uphold fair procedures for resolving conflicts. This brings us to the virtue of peace loving.

## Notes

1 Albert Schweitzer, *Philosophy of Civilization*, trans. C.T. Campion (Amherst, NY: Prometheus Books, 1987), p. 328.

2 Albert Schweitzer, *Christianity and the Religions of the World*, trans. Johanna Powers (New York: George H. Doran, 1923), p. 34; Albert Schweitzer, *A Place for Revelation: Sermons on Reverence for Life*, trans. David Larrimore Holland (New York: Irvington, 1993), pp. 48, 59.

3 Henry Clark, *The Ethical Mysticism of Albert Schweitzer* (Boston, MA: Beacon Press, 1962), p. 218, fn 17.
4 Many ethicists regard love and justice as distinct but overlapping requirements. See, for example, William K. Frankena, *Ethics*, 2nd edn (Englewood Cliffs, NJ: Prentice-Hall, 1973), p. 47.
5 Schweitzer, *Philosophy of Civilization*, p. 82. Cf. Antje Bultmann Lemke, 'Moderator's Introduction', in David C. Miller and James Pouilliard (eds), *The Relevance of Albert Schweitzer at the Dawn of the 21st Century* (Lanham, MD: University Press of America, 1992), pp. 83–4. Schweitzer apparently planned to unfold his theory of justice in the unfinished fourth volume of *The Philosophy of Civilization*, which was to be about the civilized state (Schweitzer, *Philosophy of Civilization*, p. xi).
6 Schweitzer, *Philosophy of Civilization*, p. 335.
7 Ija Pawlowska, 'How Tolerant was Albert Schweitzer?' in Miller and Pouilliard (eds), *The Relevance of Albert Schweitzer at the Dawn of the 21st Century*, p. 102.
8 Ibid., p. 101.
9 Albert Schweitzer, *Letters, 1905–1965*, trans. Joachim Neugroschel, ed. Hans Walter Bahr (New York: Macmillan, 1992), p. 288.
10 Schweitzer, *Philosophy of Civilization*, p. 340.
11 Albert Schweitzer, *Memoirs of Childhood and Youth*, trans. Kurt Bergel and Alice R. Bergel (Syracuse, NY: Syracuse University Press, 1997), p. 61.
12 James Brabazon, *Albert Schweitzer: A Biography*, 2nd edn (Syracuse, NY: Syracuse University Press, 2000), p. 485.
13 Ibid., p. 364.
14 Albert Schweitzer, 'The Ethics of Reverence for Life', *Christendom*, 1 (1936): 96. Of course, we might raise objections to the harmful effects of polygamy to women and children in other social settings.
15 Schweitzer, *A Place for Revelation*, p. 37.
16 Edgar Berman, *In Africa with Schweitzer* (New York: Harper & Row, 1986), pp. 224–5.
17 Albert Schweitzer, *Indian Thought and Its Development*, trans. Mrs Charles E.B. Russell (Gloucester, MA: Peter Smith, 1977), pp. 83–4; Albert Schweitzer, *Reverence for Life: Sermons 1909–1919*, trans. Reginald H. Fuller (New York: Irvington, 1993), p. 72.
18 Albert Schweitzer, *Primeval Forest*, trans. C.T. Campion (New York: Pyramid Books, 1961), p. 74.
19 Victor W. Sidel, 'Health Care in Exploited Societies', in Miller and Pouilliard (eds), *The Relevance of Albert Schweitzer at the Dawn of the 21st Century*, p. 64.
20 Joie Karnes, 'Applying the Ethic of Reverence for Life to the Issue of Abortion in America', in Marvin Meyer and Kurt Bergel (eds), *Reverence for Life: The Ethics of Albert Schweitzer for the Twenty-First Century* (Syracuse, NY: Syracuse University Press, 2002), pp. 295–6.
21 Schweitzer, *A Place for Revelation*, p. 66.
22 Ibid., pp. 58–85.
23 Ibid., p. 64. Cf. Albert Schweitzer, 'The Relations of the White and Coloured Races', *Contemporary Review*, 133 (1925): 65.
24 Schweitzer, *A Place for Revelation*, p. 78.
25 Ibid., p. 49.
26 Schweitzer, *Philosophy of Civilization*, p. 320.
27 John Rawls, *A Theory of Justice*, revised edn (Cambridge, MA: Harvard University Press, 1999), pp. 285–6.
28 Ibid., p. 53.
29 Schweitzer, *A Place for Revelation*, p. 74.

30 Ibid., p. 51.
31 Albert Schweitzer, *African Notebook*, trans. Mrs C.E.B. Russell (Syracuse, NY: Syracuse University Press, 2002), pp. 108–10.
32 Conrad G. Brunk, 'Restorative Justice and the Philosophical Theories of Criminal Punishment', in Michael L. Hadley (ed.), *The Spiritual Roots of Restorative Justice* (Albany, NY: State University of New York Press, 2001), pp. 31–56.
33 Schweitzer, *Reverence for Life*, p. 55; Albert Schweitzer, *Out of My Life and Thought: An Autobiography*, trans. Antje Bultmann Lemke (Baltimore, MD: Johns Hopkins University Press, 1998), p. 196; Schweitzer, *The Primeval Forest*, p. 127.
34 Schweitzer, *Philosophy of Civilization*, p. 318.
35 Schweitzer, *Letters, 1905–1965*, p. 345.
36 Schweitzer, *A Place for Revelation*, p. 46.
37 Ibid., p. 47.
38 Schweitzer, *Philosophy of Civilization*, p. 314.
39 Schweitzer, *A Place for Revelation*, p. 48.
40 Schweitzer, *Memoirs of Childhood and Youth*, pp. 13–14.
41 Edgar Berman, *In Africa with Schweitzer* (New York: Harper and Row, 1986), p. 259,
42 Schweitzer, *The Primeval Forest*, p. 90.
43 Schweitzer, 'The Relations of the White and Coloured Races', p. 68.
44 Schweitzer, *Reverence for Life*, p. 55; Schweitzer, *The Primeval Forest*, pp. 127–30.
45 Schweitzer, *Out of My Life and Thought*, p. 196.
46 See Manuel M. Davenport, 'The Moral Paternalism of Albert Schweitzer', *Ethics*, 84 (1974): 116–27.
47 Schweitzer, *Out of My Life and Thought*, p. 190.
48 Schweitzer, *The Primeval Forest*, p. 99.
49 Cf. Jackson Lee Ice, *Albert Schweitzer: Sketches for a Portrait* (Lanham, MD: University Press of America, 1994), pp. 1–8; Brabazon, *Albert Schweitzer*, pp. 371–5.
50 W.E.B. DuBois, 'The Black Man and Albert Schweitzer', in A.A. Roback (ed.), *The Albert Schweitzer Jubilee Book* (Cambridge, MA: Sci-Art, 1945), 126.
51 Schweitzer, 'The Relations of the White and Coloured Races', p. 65.
52 Ibid.
53 Ibid., p. 69.
54 Schweitzer, *Letters, 1905–1965*, p. 287.
55 Stuart Hampshire, *Justice Is Conflict* (Princeton, NJ: Princeton University Press, 2000), p. 4.

# Chapter 9

# Peace Loving and Non-Violence

> In our time, when violence clad in lies is sitting on the throne of the world, sinister as never before, I nevertheless remain convinced that truth, love, peaceableness, gentleness, and kindness are the powers above all powers.[1]

*The Philosophy of Civilization* ends with the claim that 'only such thinking as establishes the sway of the mental attitude of reverence for life can bring mankind perpetual peace.'[2] Several decades later, in protesting nuclear armaments, Schweitzer again insisted on the need for widespread inner moral change in order to achieve social peace, whether among nations, groups or individuals.[3] Peaceableness, or peace loving, is one of the ideals and virtues emphasized in reverence for life, yet only one. Peace loving implies a very strong presumption against violence, but that presumption needs to be integrated with other important ideals – including compassion and justice. Schweitzer is not the absolute pacifist he is sometimes claimed to be.

## Non-Violence

Schweitzer tends to think of peace in the same terms he describes love: 'harmony of being, community of being'.[4] Peace is the absence of angry conflict, violence and the threat of violence.[5] Accordingly, the virtue of peace loving implies removing or lessening the hatred and anger that leads to violence, often through a willingness to forgive rather than to seek revenge.[6] The mere absence of conflict, however, can signal stagnation. Pursuing moral and other ideals of excellence inevitably generates conflicts, many of which are healthy. Peace pertains to how conflicts are resolved – with justice, compassion, and without violence – rather than to the absence of conflict *per se*.

In what sense is reverence for life a form of pacifism? Douglas P. Lackey distinguishes four types of pacifism, corresponding to the following beliefs: killing is always immoral; violence (including coercion) is always immoral; violence in personal relations is always immoral but war is sometimes morally justified; and war is always immoral but sometimes personal violence is justified.[7] Lackey interprets Schweitzer as a pacifist in the first sense, that is, as someone who renounces killing under all circumstances. Because Schweitzer claims that life is sacred and that killing is always bad, Lackey understandably assumes he means that killing is never morally permissible, all things considered. He then explains why such a view is morally self-defeating. Killing is sometimes the only way to defend innocent lives, including one's own, which is a morally valuable goal.

Lackey misinterprets Schweitzer. In saying that the sacredness of life renders all killing bad, Schweitzer is affirming an ideal, not making an all-things-considered judgment that killing is never permissible in any context.[8] As we have seen, reverence for life contains myriad specific ideals that must be balanced and integrated in practical situations. Non-violence is salient among those ideals, but so is self-respect, which can justify self-defence, and so are justice and compassion, which can justify the defence of innocent third parties. Killing non-human life is often necessary in order to eat, protect ourselves, and protect innocent human lives. And killing humans, as a last desperate resort, can be necessary to protect ourselves and innocent persons against immoral aggression. Schweitzer is a pacifist in calling for active commitment to peace and non-violence, but he is not a pacifist in the sense of believing we should never defend ourselves and others by resorting to violence after seriously pursuing all other reasonable options.

Violence is to be used only when 'necessary' – to legitimately defend oneself or other innocent parties against immoral aggression. Individuals have the right to defend themselves against unjust injuries, although they should strive to be generous in forgiving.[9] Nations, too, have a right to self-defence, even in an era of weapons of mass destruction.[10] In a sermon honouring the soldiers of the First World War, Schweitzer speaks with reverence of the men and women who defended the lives and liberty of their countrymen, on both sides of the conflict.[11] His calls for world peace are not aimed at abandoning justice by having innocent people sacrifice their lives. They are calls for peace through justice, and justice sometimes requires defence of the innocent.

Perhaps the clearest indication of his views about non-violence comes in discussing *ahimsa*, the principle of non-violence and non-harm found in Hinduism, Buddhism and Jainism. He celebrates these religions, especially Jainism, for promulgating the commandment not to kill – 'one of the greatest events in the spiritual history of mankind'.[12] At the same time, he argues that *ahimsa* is initially set forth as a principle of self-purification through separation from the world.[13] Only much later is *ahimsa* rethought as a guide for engagement in the world. That guide, he contends, is less useful than reverence for life, even in the popular version of *ahimsa* practiced by Gandhi.

Had Schweitzer believed that all violence is unjustified, we would expect him to bestow unqualified praise on Gandhi for his non-violent resistance against the British in colonial India. Instead, he offers a nuanced assessment. He praises Gandhi for forcing Indian ethics 'openly to come to grips with reality' by acknowledging that the ideal of *ahimsa* cannot be fully implemented. Yet he also criticizes Gandhi for blurring *ahimsa* with non-violent resistance. *Ahimsa* is a moral ideal, whereas non-violent resistance is a particular tactic used to pursue that ideal in particular circumstances.[14] As a tactic, non-violent resistance is itself a form of force and harm, whose legitimacy needs to be assessed with regard to particular situations. There is only a 'relative' difference, not an absolute difference, between non-violent civil disobedience and more active, sometimes violent, resistance.[15]

At this point Schweitzer comes close to explicitly accepting limited violence – what he calls necessary violence that circumscribes 'the ethical' (the morally ideal). He only comes close, however, because he states the principle sympathetically for 'consideration' as an alternative to Gandhi's more thoroughgoing non-violence. The principle is that violence and other force is justified only when 'unavoidable', as a 'last expedient', directed by 'an ethical aim', and 'applied in a completely ethical disposition'.[16] This means that violence is a 'worldly' tactic that may be used only after peaceful options have been exhausted, and even then in a spirit of minimizing harm.

More fully, 'the important thing is not that only non-violent force should be employed, but that all worldly purposive action should be undertaken with the greatest possible avoidance of violence, and that ethical considerations should so dominate ourselves as to influence also the hearts of our opponents.'[17] Violence is sometimes required by self-preservation and defence of the innocent. Here as elsewhere, Schweitzer speaks for the ideal of peace, aware that violence is sometimes necessary, but he is unwilling to delineate more fully when it is justified, all things (ideals and realities) considered.

Why is Schweitzer not more straightforward about defending violence as a last resort in defending innocent life? First, his pacifism is based on ethical ideals rather than rules of duty and permissibility. Reverence for life rivets attention on non-violent solutions to problems. Schweitzer wants the focus to be on the ideal of non-violence, rather than dwelling on when our inability to achieve that ideal permits violence in pursuing other ideals such as self-respect (self-defence) and compassion and justice (in defending the innocent). As such, his pacifism does not fit neatly into Lackey's four categories, all of which are defined in terms of duties. Schweitzer's ethical idealism is simply alien to ethicists who, like Lackey, think exclusively in terms of duties and rights rather than ideals of goodness.

Second, throughout his life Schweitzer is a spokesperson for peace – for the ideal of non-violence in personal relationships and political interactions. In this role, he tends to avoid being drawn into philosophical disputes about when violence is permissible. Especially after he receives the Nobel Peace Prize for his service at Lambaréné, he is given many opportunities to speak on behalf of world peace. In doing so, he seeks to bring conflicting parties together at a time of enormous world tension by illuminating areas of common ground that form a basis for reasonable compromises.

Third, Schweitzer's acknowledgement of the need for some violence is obscured by his contrast between the ethical (as defined by morally absolute ideals) and the necessary (what is morally permissible or obligatory, all things considered). As we saw in Chapter 3, his ethical–necessity dichotomy is a misleading circumlocution, for what he means by necessity includes ethical values: specifically, legitimate self-defence and self-realization, as well as the defence of other innocent persons. Implicitly, such violence is permissible or required, albeit not ideal. Moreover, in advocating peace, Schweitzer calls for a morally-pure 'spirit of idealism' that sets itself against the power-oriented 'spirit of realism'.[18] He also says the 'spirit of reverence for life' is 'the spirit of peace', again creating the impression that all violence is immoral.[19] Nevertheless, he is keenly aware that ideals must confront reality in ways that preclude their complete attainment, and that includes the ideals of peace loving and non-violence.

For these reasons, it is understandable why Schweitzer tends to avoid explicit statements of when violence can be justified, all things considered. Nevertheless, in speaking for ideals of peace he is not a simplistic visionary. His discussions of nuclear threats reveal a voice of practical reason and decency at a time when both were in short supply.

## Commitment to World Peace

For a long time Schweitzer resisted entreaties to become involved in the increasing threat of nuclear war, fearing it would detract from his primary work as a physician and hospital administrator. He became a leading peace activist only during the last decade of his life, after receiving the Nobel Peace Prize in 1952. The transformation occurred largely because Norman Cousins visited Lambaréné and convinced Schweitzer that he could play a significant role in challenging the proliferation and testing of nuclear weapons. Nearly eighty, Schweitzer educated himself about the technical and political issues and began a series of widely-broadcast radio talks.

Defenders of nuclear deterrence appeal to its effectiveness in preventing or containing conventional warfare. They might appeal to the ideals contained in reverence for life, including justice and peace, while disagreeing with Schweitzer's personal convictions. Here is an area where an ethics of reverence for life should leave room for differences among reasonable persons in interpreting and applying moral ideals to complex practical realities. There is no doubt, however, that Schweitzer became convinced that nuclear armaments are a fundamental threat to world peace. His arguments against nuclear armaments blend common sense, science and moral appeals. He repeatedly calls for citizens and their leaders to adopt 'a change of heart' and 'a new attitude of mind: an attitude based upon ethics'.[20] The new attitude will foster mutual trust and trustworthiness.[21]

The new attitude, of course, is reverence for life, understood as an umbrella virtue and ideal that yokes together key values such as self-respect, compassion, humanitarian love, tolerance and justice – and not limited to the ideal of widening the circle to include non-human life as inherently valuable. Only two paragraphs in his published talks on nuclear weapons directly refer to reverence for all living organisms, and those passages affirm the value of life without employing technical concepts such as will-to-live and ethical mysticism.[22] This approach is not a rhetorical ploy used to attract a wider audience by focusing on peace rather than environmental ethics. It is consistent with his understanding of reverence for life as an umbrella virtue and ideal that includes many social-oriented virtues and ideals.

Love, compassion, humanitarianism and justice are the most frequent appeals in the talks protesting nuclear armaments. Justice is especially prominent, and as always it is understood primarily in terms of human rights and relationships among persons and nations. A lasting peace is possible only when human rights are applied contextually in a spirit of moral good will, so as to develop 'a just and objective solution [to conflicts] in the light of historical reality'.[23] In resolving conventional wars, special attention must be paid to property rights which, given the convoluted history of conflicts, have been blurred to the point where only reasonable compromises can redefine them.[24] The testing and proliferation of nuclear weapons threatens rights to life and to health on an unprecedented scale.[25]

Schweitzer's appeals to justice and other specific virtues were interspersed with calls for common sense and with lengthy presentations of facts. Primarily he sought to inform the public about nuclear dangers, and at the time – the McCarthy era, which was dominated by ignorance, fear and intimidation – that information was greatly needed. Schweitzer provided a lucid and calm voice which, against the background of the veneration in which he was held, was more persuasive than preaching.[26]

Even so, his approach to world peace now seems excessively individualistic. In claiming that a widespread change of attitude is what is most needed to achieve world peace, he initially underestimated the importance of negotiated peace treaties and international laws, guided by general moral principles.[27] As his views matured, however, they evolved towards the more plausible belief that treaties and laws are important but not sufficient. A widespread change in attitude is needed to prepare the way for new social structures and laws, especially international laws.[28] Reverence for life must increase in order to then be implemented, nationally and internationally, through social structures based on justice and compassion. He calls for a 'spiritual politics, to be pursued side by side with all political planning and acting. Such politics will create spiritual links among the nations.'[29]

The goal is peace among nations, not the end of nations. Schweitzer decries the 'ignoble patriotism' that elevates one's country above all others.[30] Yet he affirms the value of a 'healthful nationalism' within a broader framework of humanitarianism.[31] Emphatically, he rejects communism for perverting humanitarianism, just as he condemns fascism for perverting patriotism.[32] At the same time, he is not immune to the biases of nationalism. Edgar Berman observes, 'Germanophilia was a peculiar quirk in his otherwise magnificent mentality.'[33] There is little by way of direct condemnation of the German culture that made possible the Holocaust.

## Inner Peace

Peace loving concerns inner peace, peace within each of us, in addition to social peace. It is important not to confuse inner peace, however, with the much broader attitude of reverence for life, of which it is a part. As we have seen, reverence for life includes a host of overlapping virtues and their accompanying ideals – including compassion, justice, gratitude and peace loving, all of which contribute to both inner and social peace. When Schweitzer asserts that reverence for life promotes social peace, he is not making the simplistic claim that inner peace suffices to bring about social peace.[34]

Even so, inner peace is a significant part of reverence for life. Inner peace is not merely a psychological state of calm. Rather, it is a moral and spiritual state defined by virtues that include integrity, self-respect, resignation, serenity and hope.[35] To begin with, integrity implies wide-scoped moral commitment. In religious language, it means being in tune with God's will. For Schweitzer, that attunement centres on an ethics of self-realization and active love. In moral terms, it requires redoubling efforts to overcome 'thoughts of wickedness, thoughts of lying, thoughts of revenge and hostility'.[36] Spiritually, peace loving is the desire to live in harmony with all life. 'In the world, the [universal] will-to-life is in conflict with itself. In us – by a mystery which we do not understand – it wishes to be at peace with itself.'[37] The peace is attained through ethical mysticism – through active service in the spirit of reverence for life. It is a broadened peace defined in terms of ideals such as love, compassion and justice. Insofar as we support life, and refrain from killing, we lift ourselves above destructive conflict and achieve a unity in the universal Will to Live.

Resignation is the acceptance of realities we cannot control, including our vulnerability to suffering and death. Only some things are under our control but, as the Stoics point out, those things include our attitudes and values, at least to a considerable extent. As such, resignation is a 'profound life-affirmation' that deepens self-respect and prepares us to care more deeply for other lives.[38] Although resignation cannot remove all fear, it frees us from crippling forms of despair, suffering, anger, hatred and envy. It brings moral and spiritual serenity.

Serenity is that 'sort of happiness' which comes from knowing that spiritual values have genuine power, and from committing ourselves to their ultimate triumph.[39] At its best, serenity is the stoic assurance that the world cannot crush us.[40] In contrast with the vicissitudes of wealth, power and social status, knowing we are attuned to the good in the universe lessens our chance of being crushed by outward events.[41] Serenity is the calm from surrendering our will to the beneficent forces in the world, and in feeling supported by those forces.[42] It is not the calm that serves violent ends, as with the warriors in the *Bhagavad-Gita* who are unperturbed even in killing their relatives. Rather, it is the moral confidence that accompanies active commitment to social peace in pursuing the ideal of peace loving.[43]

Hope generates optimism, confidence and commitment. The relevant hope is the global attitude that the future will be good, as distinct from hope for specific results. And the relevant spiritual peace 'is pulsating power, not quietude'.[44] In resignation, we accept that we can never be certain of success in any specific endeavour, and accepting contingency is an important part of resignation. Nevertheless, inner peace implies the hope that overall, sometimes in ways we often do not understand, our lives will gain in meaning and we will be helped in our endeavours; somehow, things will work out. Ethical mysticism, then, defines inner peace in terms of moral engagement, unlike passive mysticism that celebrates the serenity of withdrawal.

To conclude, Schweitzer is convinced that interpersonal and international peace must emerge from moral and spiritual change. It can never be achieved by governments and treaties alone. This inner change involves commitments to justice, compassion and world peace. Peace and non-violence are essential ideals, but they must be integrated with other ideals and with practical realities. Reasonable persons might disagree about how best to make those integrations regarding complex issues such as national defence and world peace. Here, as elsewhere, reverence for life calls on each of us to engage in moral reasoning, authentically and responsibly, while respecting others who do likewise.

## Notes

1 Albert Schweitzer, *Memoirs of Childhood and Youth*, trans. Kurt Bergel and Alice R. Bergel (Syracuse, NY: Syracuse University Press, 1997), p. 95.
2 Albert Schweitzer, *Philosophy of Civilization*, trans. C.T. Campion (Amherst, NY: Prometheus Books, 1987), p. 344; cf. pp. xii, 1, 45.
3 Albert Schweitzer, *On Nuclear War and Peace*, ed. Homer A. Jack (Elgin, IL: Brethren Press, 1988), p. 40.
4 Albert Schweitzer, *A Place for Revelation: Sermons on Reverence for Life*, trans. David Larrimore Holland (New York: Irvington, 1993), pp. 7–8.
5 Schweitzer dislikes the African practice of palavers – the resolution of disputes through lively and often angry verbal interchanges and demonstrations – but today we appreciate their role in preventing violence. Albert Schweitzer, *The African Sermons*, trans. and ed. Steven E.G. Melamed, Sr (Syracuse, NY: Syracuse University Press, 2003), p. 158.
6 Schweitzer, *The African Sermons*, p. 159.
7 Douglas P. Lackey, 'Pacifism', in James E. White (ed.), *Contemporary Moral Problems*, 8th edn (Belmont, CA: Wadsworth, 2006), p. 481.
8 Cf. Henry Clark, *The Ethical Mysticism of Albert Schweitzer* (Boston, MA: Beacon Press, 1962), p. 107.
9 Schweitzer, *A Place for Revelation*, pp. 46, 48.
10 Schweitzer, *On Nuclear War and Peace*, p. 55.
11 Albert Schweitzer, *Reverence for Life: Sermons 1909–1919*, trans. Reginald H. Fuller (New York: Irvington, 1993), p. 103.
12 Albert Schweitzer, *Indian Thought and Its Development*, trans. Mrs Charles E.B. Russell (Gloucester, MA: Peter Smith, 1977), pp. 82–3.
13 Ibid., p. 80.
14 Ibid., p. 231.
15 Ibid., p. 232.
16 Ibid., pp. 233–4.
17 Ibid.
18 Albert Schweitzer, 'Religion in Modern Civilization', *Christian Century*, 51 (1 November 1934): 1483.
19 Albert Schweitzer, *Letters, 1905–1965*, trans. Joachim Neugroschel, ed. Hans Walter Bahr (New York: Macmillan, 1992), p. 331.
20 Schweitzer, *On Nuclear War and Peace*, pp. 50, 55.
21 Ibid., pp. 36–7, 39, 88, 90.
22 Ibid., pp. 38, 52.
23 Ibid., p. 45.
24 Ibid., p. 46.
25 Ibid., p. 86.
26 See James Brabazon, *Albert Schweitzer: A Biography*, 2nd edn (Syracuse, NY: Syracuse University Press, 2000), pp. 469–74.
27 Schweitzer, *Philosophy of Civilization*, p. 344. Here Schweitzer too quickly dismisses Kant's attempt to articulate peace-promoting principles in *Toward Perpetual Peace*, reprinted in Immanuel Kant, *Practical Philosophy*, trans. Mary J. Gregor, ed. Allen Wood (New York: Cambridge University Press, 1996), pp. 317–51.
28 Schweitzer, *On Nuclear War and Peace*, p. 76.
29 Albert Schweitzer, *The Teaching of Reverence for Life*, trans. Richard and Clara Winston (New York: Holt, Rinehart and Winston, 1965), p. 54.
30 Schweitzer, *Philosophy of Civilization*, p. 29.

31 Schweitzer, *On Nuclear War and Peace*, p. 54; Schweitzer, *Philosophy of Civilization*, p. 30.

32 The general issue is insightfully debated in *For Love of Country: Debating the Limits of Patriotism*, ed. Joshua Cohen (Boston, MA: Beacon Press, 1996).

33 Edgar Berman, *In Africa With Schweitzer* (New York: Harper and Row, 1986), p. 183.

34 Schweitzer, *On Nuclear War and Peace*, p. 41.

35 Henry Clark observes that inner peace is 'a state very similar to' resignation. See Clark, *The Ethical Mysticism of Albert Schweitzer*, p. 75.

36 Schweitzer, *The African Sermons*, p. 167.

37 Albert Schweitzer, 'The Problem of Ethics in the Evolution of Human Thought', in Friends of Albert Schweitzer (eds), *To Dr Albert Schweitzer: A Festschrift Commemorating His 80th Birthday* (New York: Profile Press, 1955), p. 140.

38 Schweitzer, *Philosophy of Civilization*, p. 313.

39 Ibid., p. 97.

40 Cf. Pierre Hadot, *The Inner Citadel*, trans. Michael Chase (Cambridge, MA: Harvard University Press, 1998).

41 Schweitzer, *Reverence for Life*, p. 97.

42 Ibid., p. 96.

43 Schweitzer, *Indian Thought and Its Development*, p. 186.

44 Ibid., p. 98.

# Chapter 10

# Conclusion

Search, then, for some investment for your humanity.[1]

Nietzsche called for a 'philosophical physician' who could diagnose the total health of society, indeed of humanity itself.[2] Schweitzer is such a physician, although not the one Nietzsche envisioned. 'We live in a dangerous medley of civilization and barbarism', Schweitzer writes, in which a misbalance between the 'material and spiritual has assumed a most unhealthy character'.[3] Restoring balance will require a healthy philosophy that joins self-realization to ethical idealism and nature-centred spirituality.[4] What, by way of conclusion, should we make of Schweitzer as a philosophical physician?

A physician might have varied strengths in diagnosis, aetiology and healing. As for diagnosis, Ernst Cassirer praises Schweitzer for his incisive 'medical analysis of our cultural life'. No other thinker of his generation so accurately conveys 'a strong presentiment of the crisis to come and such a clear insight into the character of this crisis'.[5] The crisis includes horrific violence on an unprecedented scale, cruelty to animals, loss of community, systemic threats to individual dignity, and collective modes of thought in the forms of uncritical nationalism, dogmatic religions and corporate shibboleths. Today the crisis also includes terrorism, dangerous technologies that outstrip moral understanding and massive environmental degradation.

As for aetiology, Schweitzer locates the primary cause of our moral sickness in spiritual decline. The decline is reflected in the thought of his contemporaries, Nietzsche and Freud, who together open the twentieth century with corrosive attacks on ethical idealism. Both these contemporaries reject humanitarian love as unrealistic and a source of excessive guilt, anxiety and depression. Their insights provide correctives to Schweitzer's sometimes excessive calls for self-perfecting, which for those of us who lack Schweitzer's exceptional moral commitment can foster unhealthy degrees of guilt. These correctives can be taken seriously, however, without overthrowing the core concepts in reverence for life. Ideals guide and inspire commitment, but they do not command impossible levels of achievement. Moral commitment is sustained by self-affirmation through service to others, rather than guilt for failures.

What about cultural healing? Schweitzer unabashedly prescribes ethical idealism as a healthy morality that advances self-fulfilment and civilization. In doing so, he calls on ethicists to develop powerfully-motivating conceptions of moral and spiritual aspiration. This vision of philosophy was out of favour when Schweitzer wrote, and even more so today. Even Cassirer, who praises Schweitzer's 'great intellectual and moral courage' in reasserting ethical idealism and attacking 'philosophical quietism', was politely silent about reverence for life as a cultural therapy.[6] Ideas get worn out,

Schweitzer observed.[7] Is that the fate of reverence for life? It should not be, once properly understood and in places revised.

Reverence for life is not a simplistic alternative to the complexity of moral reasoning. On the contrary, it integrates the full spectrum of moral ideals by understanding how they contribute to both self-realization and social progress. In doing so, it widens the circle of moral concern to include suffering creatures and life in its entirety. Ethics must be practical in two equally important ways: inspiring motivation and providing guidance. Motivation is increased as we embrace ideals that rise above minimum moral requirements. Doing so, however, does not remove the need for thoughtful balancing and integrating of competing moral ideals in response to ethical dilemmas.

Schweitzer's dichotomy between ethics and necessity has been rejected here. Or rather, it has been urged that it be rethought as a contrast between some ethical ideals (for example compassion, non-violence) and other ethical ideals (self-realization, self-defence, defence of innocent third parties). Similarly, his characterization of practical decisions as subjective should be understood in terms of permissible alternatives for individuals who authentically and responsibly exercise moral autonomy in interpreting and applying ideals. These recommendations are in tune with the emphasis on reason, realism and personal responsibility in reverence for life.

Exactly how we link morality and mental health depends on how we understand mental health, and in turn that depends on how we understand instincts and natural tendencies.[8] Freud and Nietzsche reduce all motives to self-advancement. In their view, the ideal of universal love perverts natural, exclusively self-interested desires. For Freud, health consists in satisfying sexual and aggressive instincts through socially acceptable forms of love and work.[9] For Nietzsche, health consists of self-reverence, self-mastery and vitality.[10] Pathology arises from suppressing the instincts of will to power (Nietzsche) and sex and aggression (Freud) through the inner tyrannies of the superego's cultural ideal of universal love. Schweitzer's ethics begins with a far more optimistic assessment of human instincts. Aggression, yes, but also desires for personal growth and empathy for others.

More recent psychologists interested in moral matters are closer to Schweitzer's themes, and philosophers do well to attend to what health psychologists have to say (and *vice versa*). Since Schweitzer wrote, humanistic psychologists like Erich Fromm and Abraham Maslow appreciated this interweaving of morality and mental health. Today, the movement called positive psychology is developing connections between morality and mental health within a scientific framework.[11] Like Schweitzer, positive psychologists emphasize authenticity, love, optimism and creative self-realization. Like Schweitzer, they set themselves against the egoism of Nietzsche and Freud, and they develop more promising conceptions of human nature and health. Yes, we have destructive tendencies, but we also have natural desires to connect our lives with others in sharing, sympathetic and supportive ways, as manifested in common decency and authentic projects of love. As a result, morality is a natural expression of our will to live. Our moral strategy should be to connect our limited sympathetic instincts to the much stronger drives for self-realization and meaning. Moral health resides in the interpenetration of these natural desires. The self is salient, but only against the background of ideals of respect for others, including respect for the natural environment.

Of course, Schweitzer's ethics and spirituality transcend psychology. Schweitzer is an ethical idealist who systematically nudges moral values in a spiritual direction rooted in the sacredness of life. Although he remains a practical idealist, attuned to the exigencies of context, he is confident that moral ideals 'are the powers above all powers'.[12] Ideals constitute the best of humanity, and they have the power to transform individuals and societies. Civilization is inherently ethical, once we understand it as 'the sum total of all progress … in so far as this progress helps towards the spiritual perfecting of individuals'.[13] This spiritual self-realization just is moral endeavour, but it involves all sound values. All values – including aesthetic, religious, scientific, technological and economic values – have moral and spiritual implications insofar as they contribute to self-perfecting. We can be optimistic and hopeful in our willing, despite being pessimistic in much of what we know about the world.[14]

Finally, Schweitzer sustains a creative tension between mandatory high ideals and maximum individual freedom in interpreting and applying ideals. More than most ethicists, he trusts individuals to embody moral ideals in their lives in myriad ways. As such, reverence for life is a pluralistic, ecumenical, broadly tolerant moral perspective. Even so, few philosophers any longer believe that any one moral perspective will appeal to every morally concerned and responsible individual. There is no canonical ethical theory. Moral and spiritual thought is central to civilization, but diverse moral and spiritual perspectives have always shaped civilization.

Much common ground remains, however, and reverence for life helps identify it. Reverence for life yokes together all reasonable values as contributing to development of life. In doing so, it especially highlights the ideals of authenticity, compassion, gratitude, justice and peace. It invites us to build on natural desires for self-development and empathy, and to continually widen the circle of our moral concern as part of being at home in the universe. And it inspires us to undertake projects of love through which we experience unity with life. Ethics begins from within, unfolds in self-realization, and finds completion in an ever-widening community of love.

## Notes

1 Albert Schweitzer, *Philosophy of Civilization*, trans. C.T. Campion (Amherst, NY: Prometheus Books, 1987), p. 322.
2 Friedrich Nietzsche, *The Gay Science*, trans. Walter Kaufmann (New York: Vintage Books, 1974), p. 35.
3 Schweitzer, *Philosophy of Civilization*, pp. 1, 21.
4 Ibid., p. 3.
5 Ernst Cassirer, 'Albert Schweitzer as Critic of Nineteenth-Century Ethics', in A.A. Roback (ed.), *The Albert Schweitzer Jubilee Book* (Cambridge, MA: Sci-Art, 1945), p. 242.
6 Ibid., p. 257.
7 Schweitzer, *Philosophy of Civilization*, p. 42.
8 Cf. Rem Edwards, 'Introduction', in *Ethics of Psychiatry*, ed. Rem Edwards (Amherst, NY: Prometheus Books, 1997), p. 17. See also Mike W. Martin, *From Morality to Mental Health: Virtue and Vice in a Therapeutic Culture* (New York: Oxford University Press, 2006).

9 Sigmund Freud, *Civilization and Its Discontents*, trans. James Strachey (New York: W.W. Norton, 1961), pp. 10–21; and *The Future of an Illusion*, trans. James Strachey (New York: W.W. Norton, 1961).

10 Friedrich Nietzsche, *On the Genealogy of Morality*, trans. Maudemarie Clark and Alan J. Swensen (Indianapolis, IN: Hackett, 1998).

11 See, for example, C.R. Snyder and Shane J. Lopez (eds), *Handbook of Positive Psychology* (New York: Oxford University Press, 2002); and Christopher Peterson and Martin E.P. Seligman (eds), *Character Strengths and Virtues: A Handbook and Classification* (New York: Oxford University Press, 2004).

12 Albert Schweitzer, *Memoirs of Childhood and Youth*, trans. Kurt Bergel and Alice R. Bergel (Syracuse, NY: Syracuse University Press), p. 95.

13 Schweitzer, *Philosophy of Civilization*, pp. 91, 57.

14 Albert Schweitzer, *Out of My Life and Thought*, trans. Antje Bultmann Lemke (Baltimore, MD: Johns Hopkins University Press, 1998), p. 242.

# Bibliography

## Albert Schweitzer's Writings, Selected


*African Notebook*, trans. Mrs C.E.B. Russell (Syracuse, NY: Syracuse University Press, 2003).

*The African Sermons*, trans. and ed. Steven E.G. Melamed, Sr (Syracuse, NY: Syracuse University Press, 2003).

*Albert Schweitzer: An Anthology*, ed. Charles R. Joy (Boston, MA: Beacon Press, 1947).

*The Albert Schweitzer–Hélène Bresslau Letters, 1902–1912*, trans. Antje Bultmann Lemke, ed. Rhena Schweitzer Miller and Gustav Woytt (Syracuse, NY: Syracuse University Press, 2003).

*The Animal World of Albert Schweitzer*, trans. and ed. Charles R. Joy (Boston, MA: Beacon Press, 1950).

'Aus meinem Leben: Ein Vortrag', *Schweitzer Monatshefte*, 50 (1970): 1–7.

'Busy Days in Lambaréné', *Christian Century*, 51 (14 March 1934): 355–7.

*Christianity and the Religions of the World*, trans. Johanna Powers (New York: George H. Doran, 1923).

'The Correspondence between Bertrand Russell and Albert Schweitzer', ed. Herbert Spiegelberg, *International Studies in Philosophy*, 12 (1980): 1–45.

*The Essence of Faith: Philosophy of Religion*, trans. Kurt F. Leidecker (New York: Philosophical Library, 1966).

'The Ethics of Reverence for Life', *Christendom*, 1 (1936): 225–39.

*The Forest Hospital at Lambaréné* (New York: Henry Holt, 1931).

*Goethe: Five Studies*, trans. Charles R. Joy (Boston, MA: Beacon Press, 1961).

*Indian Thought and Its Development*, trans. Mrs Charles E.B. Russell (Gloucester, MA: Peter Smith, 1977). Copyright 1936 by the Beacon Press.

*J.S. Bach*, trans. Ernest Newman (2 vols, New York: Dover Publications, 1966).

*Letters, 1905–1965*, trans. Joachim Neugroschel, ed. Hans Walter Bahr (New York: Macmillan, 1992).

*Memoirs of Childhood and Youth*, trans. Kurt Bergel and Alice R. Bergel (Syracuse, NY: Syracuse University Press, 1997).

*The Mystery of the Kingdom of God: The Secret of Jesus' Messiahship and Passion*, trans. Walter Lowrie (Amherst, NY: Prometheus Books, 1985).

*The Mysticism of Paul the Apostle*, trans. William Montgomery (Baltimore, MD: Johns Hopkins University Press, 1998).

*On Nuclear War and Peace*, ed. Homer A. Jack (Elgin, IL: Brethren Press, 1988).

*Out of My Life and Thought: An Autobiography*, trans. Antje Bultmann Lemke (Baltimore, MD: Johns Hopkins University Press, 1998). Copyright 1990 by Henry Holt and Company.

*The Philosophy of Civilization*, trans. C.T. Campion (Amherst, NY: Prometheus Books, 1987). Contains two volumes: *The Decay and Restoration of Civilization*, and *Civilization and Ethics*. Copyright 1987 by Rhena Schweitzer Miller.

*A Place for Revelation: Sermons on Reverence for Life*, trans. David Larrimore Holland (New York: Irvington, 1993).

*The Primeval Forest*, trans. C.T. Campion (New York: Pyramid Books, 1963). Copyright 1931 by Macmillan. Reprinted, with same pagination, by the Johns Hopkins University Press, 1998. Contains *On the Edge of the Primeval Forest*, and *More from the Primeval Forest*.

'The Problem of Ethics in the Evolution of Human Thought', in Friends of Albert Schweitzer (eds), *To Dr Albert Schweitzer: A Festschrift Commemorating His 80th Birthday* (New York: Profile Press, 1955), pp. 125–40.

*The Psychiatric Study of Jesus: Exposition and Criticism*, trans. Charles R. Joy (Gloucester, MA: Peter Smith, 1975).

*The Quest of the Historical Jesus*, trans. W. Montgomery, J.R. Coates, Susan Cupitt and John Bowden, ed. John Bowden (Minneapolis, MN: Fortress Press, 2001).

'The Relations of the White and Coloured Races', *Contemporary Review*, 133 (1925): 65–70.

'Religion and Modern Civilization', *Christian Century*, 51 (28 November 1934): 1519–21.

'Religion in Modern Civilization', *Christian Century*, 51 (1 November 1934): 1483–4.

*Reverence for Life: Sermons 1909–1919*, trans. Reginald H. Fuller (New York: Irvington, 1993).

*The Spiritual Life: Selected Writings of Albert Schweitzer*, ed. Charles R. Joy (Hopewell, NJ: Ecco Press, 1947).

*The Story of My Pelican*, trans. Martha Wardenburg (London: Souvenir, 1964).

'Sunday at Lambaréné', *Christian Century*, 48 (March 1931): 373–6.

*The Teaching of Reverence for Life*, trans. Richard and Clara Winston (New York: Holt, Rinehart and Winston, 1965).

*A Treasury of Albert Schweitzer*, ed. Thomas Kiernan (New York: Gramercy Books, 1994).

'Your Second Job', *Readers Digest*, 55 (October 1949): 1–5.

### Additional Sources

Armstrong, Susan J., and Richard G. Botzler (eds), *Environmental Ethics* (New York: McGraw-Hill, 1993).

Arneson, Richard J., 'The Principle of Fairness and Free Rider Problems', *Ethics*, 92 (1982): 617–33.

Attfield, Robin, *The Ethics of Environmental Concern* (Oxford: Blackwell, 1983).

Barsam, Ara Paul, 'Albert Schweitzer, Jainism, and Reverence for Life', in Marvin Meyer and Kurt Bergel (eds), *Reverence for Life: The Ethics of Albert Schweitzer for the Twenty-First Century* (Syracuse, NY: Syracuse University Press, 2002).

Becker, Lawrence C., *Reciprocity* (New York: Routledge and Kegan Paul, 1986).

Bellah, Robert N., Richard Madsen, William M. Sullivan, Ann Swidler and Steven M. Tipton, *Habits of the Heart: Individualism and Commitment in American Life* (Berkeley, CA: University of California Press, 1985).

Bentley, James, *Albert Schweitzer: The Enigma* (New York: HarperCollins, 1992).

Bergel, Kurt, 'Albert Schweitzer's Reverence for Life', *The Humanist*, 6 (1946): 31–4.

Berger, Fred R., 'Gratitude', *Ethics*, 85 (1974/75): 299.

Berman, Edgar, *In Africa with Schweitzer* (New York: Harper and Row, 1986).

Bixler, J.S., 'Productive Tensions in the Work of Albert Schweitzer', in A.A. Roback (ed.), *The Albert Schweitzer Jubilee Book* (Cambridge, MA: Sci-Art, 1945), pp. 71–86.

Bourke, Vernon J., 'Albert Schweitzer's Ethical Principles', *Journal of Value Inquiry*, 11 (1977): 41–3.

Brabazon, James, *Albert Schweitzer: A Biography*, 2nd edn (Syracuse, NY: Syracuse University Press, 2000).

Brunk, Conrad G., 'Restorative Justice and the Philosophical Theories of Criminal Punishment', in Michael L. Hadley (ed.), *The Spiritual Roots of Restorative Justice* (Albany, NY: State University of New York Press, 2001), pp. 31–56.

Callicott, J. Baird, 'On the Intrinsic Value of Nonhuman Species', in Bryan G. Norton (ed.), *The Preservation of the Species: The Value of Biological Diversity* (Princeton, NJ: Princeton University Press, 1986) pp. 138–172.

Camenisch, Paul F., 'Gift and Gratitude in Ethics', *Journal of Religious Ethics*, 9 (1981): 1–34.

Card, Claudia, 'Gratitude and Obligation', *American Philosophical Quarterly*, 25 (1988): 115–27.

Carson, Rachel, *Silent Spring* (Boston, MA: Houghton Mifflin, 1962).

Cassirer, Ernst, 'Albert Schweitzer as Critic of Nineteenth-Century Ethics', in A.A. Roback (ed.), *The Albert Schweitzer Jubilee Book* (Cambridge, MA: Sci-Art, 1945), pp. 241–57.

Cavell, Stanley, *Conditions Handsome and Unhandsome: The Constitution of Emersonian Perfectionism* (Chicago, IL: University of Chicago Press, 1990).

Clark, Henry, *The Ethical Mysticism of Albert Schweitzer* (Boston, MA: Beacon Press, 1962). Also published as *The Philosophy of Albert Schweitzer* (London: Methuen, 1964).

Cohen, Joshua (ed.), *For Love of Country: Debating the Limits of Patriotism* (Boston, MA: Beacon Press, 1996).

Colby, Anne, and William Damon, *Some Do Care: Contemporary Lives of Moral Commitment* (New York: Free Press, 1992).

Cooper, David E., *The Measure of Things: Humanism, Humility, and Mystery* (Oxford: Clarendon, 2002).

Cousins, Norman, *Albert Schweitzer's Mission: Healing and Peace* (New York: W.W. Norton, 1985).

Cox, Gray, *The Ways of Peace* (New York: Paulist Press, 1986).

Crosby, Donald A., *A Religion of Nature* (Albany, NY: State University of New York Press, 2002).

Danto, Arthur C., *Mysticism and Morality: Oriental Thought and Moral Philosophy* (New York: Columbia University Press, 1988).

Davenport, Manuel M., 'The Moral Paternalism of Albert Schweitzer', *Ethics*, 84 (1974): 116–27.

——, 'The Aesthetic Foundation of Schweitzer's Ethics', *Southwestern Journal of Philosophy*, 5 (spring 1994): 39–46.

DesJardins, Joseph R., *Environmental Ethics: An Introduction to Environmental Philosophy*, 4th edn (Belmont, CA: Wadsworth, 2006).

Dewey, John, *Human Nature and Conduct* (New York: Modern Library, 1977 [1922]).

Dickens, Charles, *Bleak House* (New York: Bantam, 1983).

Doyle, James F., 'Schweitzer's Extension of Ethics to All Life', *Journal of Value Inquiry*, 11 (1977): 43–6.

DuBois, W.E.B., 'The Black Man and Albert Schweitzer', in A.A. Roback (ed.), *The Albert Schweitzer Jubilee Book* (Cambridge, MA: Sci-Art, 1945), pp. 121–7.

Edwards, Rem, 'Introduction', in Rem Edwards (ed.), *Ethics of Psychiatry* (Amherst, NY: Prometheus Books, 1997).

Eiseley, Loren, *The Star Thrower* (San Diego, CA: Harcourt Brace, 1978).

Emmons, Robert A., and Michael E. McCullough (eds), *The Psychology of Gratitude* (New York: Oxford University Press, 2004).

Epictetus, *The Handbook* (*The Encheiridion*), trans. Nicholas P. White (Indianapolis, IN: Hackett, 1983).

Evans, J. Claude, *With Respect for Nature* (Albany, NY: State University of New York Press, 2005).

Fisher, John A., 'Taking Sympathy Seriously: A Defense of Our Moral Psychology Toward Animals', in Eugene C. Hargrove (ed.), *The Animal Rights/Environmental Ethics Debate: The Environmental Perspective* (Albany, NY: State University of New York Press, 1992), pp. 227–48.

Franck, Frederick, *My Days with Albert Schweitzer: A Lambaréné Landscape* (New York: Lyons and Burford, 1959).

Frank, Arthur W., *The Wounded Storyteller* (Chicago, IL: University of Chicago Press, 1995).

——, *The Renewal of Generosity: Illness, Medicine, and How to Live* (Chicago, IL: University of Chicago Press, 2004).

Frankena, William K., *Ethics*, 2nd edn (Englewood Cliffs, NJ: Prentice-Hall, 1973).

Frankfurt, Harry G., *The Reasons of Love* (Princeton, NJ: Princeton University Press, 2004).

Free, Ann Cottrell, *Animals, Nature and Albert Schweitzer* (Washington, DC: Flying Fox Press, 1988).

Freud, Sigmund, *Civilization and Its Discontents*, trans. James Strachey (New York: W.W. Norton, 1961).

——, *The Future of an Illusion*, trans. James Strachey (New York: W.W. Norton, 1961).

Friends of Albert Schweitzer (eds), *To Dr Albert Schweitzer: A Festschrift Commemorating His 80th Birthday* (New York: Profile Press, 1955).

Gell, C.W.M., 'Schweitzer and Radhakrishnan: A Comparison', *Hibbert Journal*, 51 (1952/1953): 355–65.

——, 'Dr Schweitzer: A Re-Assessment', *Hibbert Journal*, 55 (1956/1957): 330–34.

Gewirth, Alan, *Self-Fulfillment* (Princeton, NJ: Princeton University Press, 1998).

Gier, Nicholas F., *The Virtue of Nonviolence: From Gautama to Gandhi* (Albany, NY: State University of New York Press, 2004).

Goodpaster, Kenneth E., 'On Being Morally Considerable', *Journal of Philosophy*, 75 (1978): 308–25.

Griffith, Nancy Snell, and Laura Person, *Albert Schweitzer: An International Bibliography* (Boston, MA: G.K. Hall and Co., 1981).

Hadot, Pierre, *The Inner Citadel*, trans. Michael Chase (Cambridge, MA: Harvard University Press, 1998).

Hampshire, Stuart, *Justice Is Conflict* (Princeton, NJ: Princeton University Press, 2000).

Hill, Thomas E., 'Ideals of Human Excellence and Preserving Natural Environments', in Thomas E. Hill, *Autonomy and Self-Respect* (New York: Cambridge University Press, 1991), pp. 104–17.

Hobbes, Thomas, 'On Human Nature', in *The English Works of Thomas Hobbes* (London, 1845), Vol. IV, ch. 9.

Hogg, A.G., 'The Ethical Teaching of Dr Schweitzer', *International Review of Missions*, 4 (April 1925): 237–51.

Horgan, John, *Rational Mysticism* (New York: Houghton Mifflin, 2003).

Hunnex, Milton D., 'Mysticism and Ethics: Radhakrishnan and Schweitzer', *Philosophy East and West*, 8 (October 1958/January 1959): 121–36.

Hurka, Thomas, *Perfectionism* (New York: Oxford University Press, 1993).

Ice, Jackson Lee, *Schweitzer: Prophet of Radical Theology* (Philadelphia, PA: Westminster Press, 1971).

——, *Albert Schweitzer: Sketches for a Portrait* (Lanham, MD: University Press of America, 1994).

Jenni, Kathie, 'Vices of Inattention', *Journal of Applied Philosophy*, 20:3 (2003): 279–95.

Jilek-Aall, Louise, *Working with Dr Schweitzer: Sharing His Reverence for Life* (Blaine, WA: Hancock House, 1990).

Johnson, Lawrence E., *A Morally Deep World* (New York: Cambridge University Press, 1991).

Kant, Immanuel, 'Toward Perpetual Peace', in Immanuel Kant, *Practical Philosophy*, trans. Mary J. Gregor, ed. Allen Wood (New York: Cambridge University Press, 1996), pp. 317–51.

Karefa-Smart, John A.M., 'Albert Schweitzer, Physician', in David C. Miller and James Pouilliard (eds), *The Relevance of Albert Schweitzer at the Dawn of the 21st Century* (Lanham, MD: University Press of America, 1992).

Karnes, Joie, 'Applying the Ethic of Reverence for Life to the Issue of Abortion in America', in Marvin Meyer and Kurt Bergel (eds), *Reverence for Life: The Ethics of Albert Schweitzer for the Twenty-First Century* (Syracuse, NY: Syracuse University Press, 2002), pp. 291–6.

Keller, Evelyn Fox, *A Feeling for the Organism: The Life and Work of Barbara McClintock* (New York: W.H. Freeman and Company, 1983).
Kleinig, John, *Valuing Life* (Princeton, NJ: Princeton University Press, 1991).
Kohak, Erazim, *The Green Halo: A Bird's-Eye View of Ecological Ethics* (Chicago, IL: Open Court, 2000).
Kohn, Alfie, *The Brighter Side of Human Nature* (New York: Basic Books, 1990).
Kraus, Oskar, *Albert Schweitzer: His Work and His Philosophy* (London: Adam and Charles Black, 1944).
Lackey, Douglas P., 'Pacifism', in James E. White (ed.), *Contemporary Moral Problems*, 8th edn (Belmont, CA: Wadsworth, 2006), pp. 480–93.
Langfeldt, Gabriel, *Albert Schweitzer: A Study of His Philosophy of Life* (London: George Allen and Unwin, 1960).
Lemke, Antje Bultmann, 'Moderator's Introduction', in David C. Miller and James Pouilliard (eds), *The Relevance of Albert Schweitzer at the Dawn of the 21st Century* (Lanham, MD: University Press of America, 1992), pp. 83–4.
Levin, Jessica, 'In the Heart of Sickness: A Life Portrait of Dr Albert Schweitzer', in Daniel M. Mengara (ed.), *Images of Africa: Stereotypes and Realities* (Trenton, NJ: Africa World Press, 2001), pp. 237–48.
McConnell, Terrance, *Gratitude* (Philadelphia, PA: Temple University Press, 1993).
MacIntyre, Alasdair, *After Virtue*, 2nd edn (Notre Dame, IN: University of Notre Dame Press, 1984).
McMahan, Jeff, *The Ethics of Killing: Problems at the Margins of Life* (New York: Oxford University Press, 2002).
Marietta, Don E., 'Environmental Holism and Individuals', *Environmental Ethics*, 10 (1988): 251–8.
Marshall, George, and David Poling, *Schweitzer: A Biography* (Baltimore, MD: Johns Hopkins University Press, 2000).
Martin, Mike W., 'Rethinking Reverence for Life', *Between the Species*, 9 (1993): 204–13.
——, *Virtuous Giving: Philanthropy, Voluntary Service, and Caring* (Bloomington, IN: Indiana University Press, 1994).
——, 'Good Fortune Obligates: Gratitude, Philanthropy, and Colonialism', *Southern Journal of Philosophy*, 37 (1999): 57–75.
——, *Meaningful Work: Rethinking Professional Ethics* (New York: Oxford University Press, 2000).
——, *From Morality to Mental Health: Virtue and Vice in a Therapeutic Culture* (New York: Oxford University Press, 2006).
Mengara, Daniel M. (ed.), *Images of Africa: Stereotypes and Realities* (Trenton, NJ: Africa World Press, 2001).
Meyer, Marvin, 'Albert Schweitzer and the Image of Jesus in the Gospel of Thomas', in Marvin Meyer and Charles Hughes (eds) *Jesus Then and Now: Images of Jesus in History and Christology* (Harrisburg, PA: Trinity Press International, 2001), pp. 72–90.
——, and Kurt Bergel (eds), *Reverence for Life: The Ethics of Albert Schweitzer for the Twenty-First Century* (Syracuse, NY: Syracuse University Press, 2002).

Miller, David C., and James Pouilliard (eds), *The Relevance of Albert Schweitzer at the Dawn of the 21st Century* (Lanham, MD: University Press of America, 1992).

Morrison, Toni, *Song of Solomon* (New York: New American Library, 1977).

Mumford, Lewis, *The Conduct of Life* (New York: Harcourt Brace Jovanovich, 1970).

Murdoch, Iris, *The Sovereignty of Good* (London: Ark Paperbacks, 1985).

Nietzsche, Friedrich, *The Gay Science*, trans. Walter Kaufmann (New York: Vintage Books, 1974).

——, *On the Genealogy of Morality*, trans. Maudemarie Clark and Alan J. Swensen (Indianapolis, IN: Hackett, 1998).

Nozick, Robert, *Anarchy, State, and Utopia* (New York: Basic Books, 1974).

——, *Philosophical Explanations* (Cambridge, MA: Harvard University Press, 1981).

O'Connor, John, 'Philanthropy and Selfishness', in Ellen Frankel Paul, Fred. D. Miller, Jr, Jeffrey Paul and John Ahrens (eds), *Beneficence, Philanthropy and the Public Good* (Oxford: Blackwell, 1987), pp. 113–27.

Pagels, Elaine, *Beyond Belief* (New York: Random House, 2003).

Park, O'Hyun, 'Hinduism in Perspective', in Ninian Smart and B. Srinivasa Murthy (eds), *East–West Encounters in Philosophy and Religion* (Long Beach, CA: Long Beach Publications, 1996), pp. 234–44.

Passmore, John A., *Man's Responsibility for Nature* (New York: Scribners, 1974).

Pawlowska, Ija, 'How Tolerant was Albert Schweitzer?', in David C. Miller and James Pouilliard (eds), *The Relevance of Albert Schweitzer at the Dawn of the 21st Century* (Lanham, MD: University Press of America, 1992), pp. 99–103.

Payton, Robert, 'American Values and Private Philanthropy', in Kenneth W. Thompson (ed.), *Philanthropy: Private Means, Public Ends* (Lanham, MD: University Press of America, 1987), pp. 3–20.

Pellegrino, Edmund D., and David C. Thomasma, *The Virtues in Medical Practice* (New York: Oxford University Press, 1993).

Peterson, Christopher, and Martin E.P. Seligman (eds), *Character Strengths and Virtues: A Handbook and Classification* (New York: Oxford University Press, 2004).

Picht, Werner, *The Life and Thought of Albert Schweitzer*, trans. Edward Fitzgerald (New York: Harper and Row, 1964).

Pike, Nelson, *Mystic Union* (Ithaca, NY: Cornell University Press, 1992).

Pincoffs, Edmund L., *Quandaries and Virtues* (Lawrence, KS: University Press of Kansas, 1986).

Pojman, Louis P. (ed.), *Environmental Ethics: Readings in Theory and Application* (Boston, MA: Jones and Bartlett, 1994).

Powell, Mark Allan, *Jesus as a Figure in History* (Louisville, KY: Westminster John Knox Press, 1998).

Puka, Bill, *Toward Moral Perfectionism* (New York: Garland, 1990).

Putnam, Hilary, *The Collapse of the Fact/Value Dichotomy and Other Essays* (Cambridge, MA: Harvard University Press, 2002).

Rachels, James, *The Elements of Moral Philosophy*, 4th edn (New York: McGraw-Hill, 2003).

Rawls, John, *A Theory of Justice*, revised edn (Cambridge, MA: Harvard University Press, 1999).

Regan, Tom, *The Case for Animal Rights*, updated edn (Berkeley, CA: University of California Press, 2004).

——, and Peter Singer (eds), *Animal Rights and Human Obligations*, 2nd edn (Englewood Cliffs, NJ: Prentice Hall, 1989).

Rescher, Nicholas, *Ethical Idealism* (Berkeley, CA: University of California Press, 1987).

Rienaecker, Victor, *Albert Schweitzer* (London: Murray, Edwards and Co., 1963).

Roback, A.A. (ed.), *The Albert Schweitzer Jubilee Book* (Cambridge, MA: Sci-Art, 1945).

Roberts, Robert C., and W. Jay Wood, 'Humility and Epistemic Goods', in Michael DePaul and Linda Zagzebski (eds) *Intellectual Virtue* (Oxford: Clarendon, 2003), pp. 257–79.

Rogers, Ben (ed.), *Is Nothing Sacred?* (New York: Routledge, 2004).

Roof, Wade Clark, *Spiritual Marketplace: Baby Boomers and the Remaking of American Religion* (Princeton, NJ: Princeton University Press, 1992).

Sartre, Jean-Paul, *The Words*, trans. Bernard Frechtman (Greenwich, CT: Fawcett, 1964).

——, *Being and Nothingness*, trans. Hazel E. Barnes (New York: Washington Square Press, 1966).

——, 'Existentialism is a Humanism', in Walter Kaufmann (ed.), *Existentialism from Dostoevsky to Sartre* (New York: New American Library, 1975).

Schopenhauer, Arthur, *The World as Will and Representation*, trans. E.F.J. Payne (2 vols, New York: Dover Publications, 1966).

Schrift, Alan D. (ed.), *The Logic of the Gift: Toward an Ethic of Generosity* (New York: Routledge, 1997).

Seaver, George, *Albert Schweitzer: The Man and His Mind*, 5th edn (London: Adam and Charles Black, 1959).

Sen, Amartya, *On Ethics and Economics* (Oxford: Blackwell, 1987).

Sidel, Victor W., 'Health Care in Exploited Societies', in David C. Miller and James Pouilliard (eds), *The Relevance of Albert Schweitzer at the Dawn of the 21st Century* (Lanham, MD: University Press of America, 1992), pp. 63–71.

Singer, Peter, *Writings on an Ethical Life* (New York: HarperCollins, 2000).

Skrbina, David, *Panpsychism in the West* (Cambridge, MA: MIT Press, 2005).

Smith, T.G., 'Reiner on the Future of Schweitzer's Ethics', *Journal of Value Inquiry*, 5 (1971): 131–5.

Snyder, C.R., and Shane J. Lopez (eds), *Handbook of Positive Psychology* (New York: Oxford University Press, 2002).

Spiegelberg, Herbert, 'Good Fortune Obligates: Albert Schweitzer's Second Ethical Principle', *Ethics*, 85 (1975): 227–34.

——, 'A Defense of Human Equality', in *Steppingstones Toward an Ethics for Fellow Existers* (Dordrecht: Martinus Nijhoff, 1986), pp. 131–53.

Suzuki, David, *The Sacred Balance: Rediscovering Our Place in Nature* (Vancouver: Greystone Books, 2002).

Taylor, Charles, *The Ethics of Authenticity* (Cambridge, MA: Harvard University Press, 1992).

——, *Varieties of Religion Today: William James Revisited* (Cambridge, MA: Harvard University Press, 2002).

Taylor, Paul, *Respect for Nature* (Princeton, NJ: Princeton University Press, 1986).

Taylor, Shelley E., *The Tending Instinct* (New York: Henry Holt and Company, 2002).

Tillich, Paul, *The Courage to Be*, 2nd edn (New Haven, CT: Yale University Press, 2000).

Trianosky, Gregory W., 'Virtue, Action, and the Good Life: Toward a Theory of the Virtues', *Pacific Philosophical Quarterly*, 68 (1987): 124–47.

Varner, Gary E., *In Nature's Interests?: Interests, Animal Rights, and Environmental Ethics* (New York: Oxford University Press, 1998).

Visscher, Maurice B., 'A Humanist View of Reverence for All Life', *Religious Humanism*, 7:4 (autumn, 1973): 152–5.

Wallace, James D., *Moral Relevance and Moral Conflict* (Ithaca, NY: Cornell University Press, 1988).

Warren, Mary Anne, *Moral Status: Obligations to Persons and Other Living Things* (New York: Oxford University Press, 1997).

Wellman, Carl, 'An Analysis of Reverence for Life', *Journal of Value Inquiry*, 11 (1977): 46–8.

Williams, Bernard, 'A Critique of Utilitarianism', in J.J.C. Smart and Bernard Williams, *Utilitarianism: For and Against* (New York: Cambridge University Press, 1973).

——, *Moral Luck* (Cambridge: Cambridge University Press, 1981).

Wilson, Edward O., *Biophilia* (Cambridge, MA: Harvard University Press, 1984).

——, *The Future of Life* (New York: Vintage Books, 2002).

Wolf, Susan, 'Moral Saints', *Journal of Philosophy*, 79:8 (August 1982): 419–39.

Woodruff, Paul, *Reverence: Renewing a Forgotten Virtue* (New York: Oxford University Press, 2001).

# Index